CW00432667

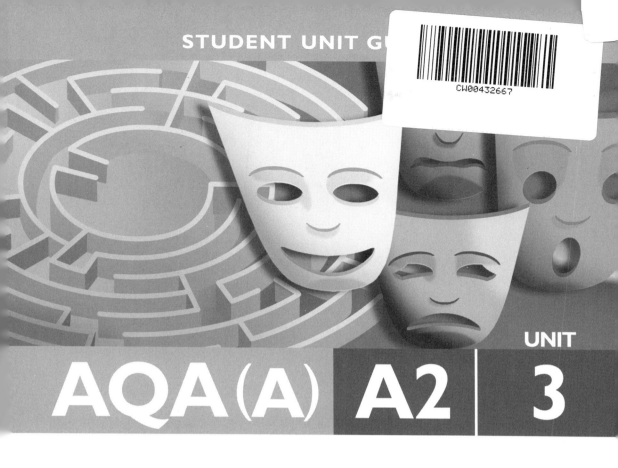

AQA (A) A2 | UNIT 3

Psychology

Topics in Psychology (1):
Intelligence and Learning, Eating Behaviour,
Perception and Gender

Jean-Marc Lawton

Philip Allan Updates, an imprint of Hodder Education, an Hachette UK company, Market Place, Deddington, Oxfordshire OX15 0SE

Orders
Bookpoint Ltd, 130 Milton Park, Abingdon, Oxfordshire OX14 4SB
tel: 01235 827720
fax: 01235 400454
e-mail: uk.orders@bookpoint.co.uk

Lines are open 9.00 a.m.–5.00 p.m., Monday to Saturday, with a 24-hour message answering service. You can also order through the Philip Allan Updates website: www.philipallan.co.uk

© Philip Allan Updates 2009

ISBN 978-0-340-99176-3

First printed 2009
Impression number 5 4 3 2 1
Year 2014 2013 2012 2011 2010 2009

This guide has been written specifically to support students preparing for the AQA Specification A A2 Psychology Unit 3 examination. The content has been neither approved nor endorsed by AQA and remains the sole responsibility of the author.

Typeset by Phoenix Photosetting, Chatham, Kent
Printed by MPG Books, Bodmin

Hachette UK's policy is to use papers that are natural, renewable and recyclable products and made from wood grown in sustainable forests. The logging and manufacturing processes are expected to conform to the environmental regulations of the country of origin.

Contents

Introduction

■ ■ ■

Content Guidance

■ ■ ■

Questions and Answers

Introduction

About this guide

This guide will help you prepare for the AQA(A) A2 Psychology Unit 3 examination. Four of the eight topics in Unit 3 are covered in this guide. (The other four topics are covered in a second book, AQA(A) A2 Psychology, Unit 3: Topics in Psychology (2), ISBN 978-0-340-99175-6.) This publication is not intended as a revision guide or textbook, but rather as a support device to revision and learning. Therefore, this guide looks first at the specification content and how it is examined and second at how answers of varying quality are assessed.

- The specification content for each topic is fully explained so that you understand what would be required from you in your examination (although other content may be equally appropriate).
- Content appropriate to each topic is outlined, to an extent that it would be possible to construct an answer to questions set on that topic.
- A sample question for each topic is provided, along with an explanation of its requirements.
- Sample answers are also provided, along with examiner comments explaining the strengths and limitations of each answer.

Using this guide

You can use this guide in a variety of ways.

- **During your course,** each time you start a new topic, e.g. in eating behaviour, use the unit guide to give you a quick overview of what is involved; re-read each topic at regular intervals as you are studying it in class.
- **When you start revising,** use the unit guide to review the specification areas you have studied, (such as eating disorders). Use the unit guide to refresh your learning and consolidate your knowledge of each of the four Unit 3 topics covered.
- **When practising for the examination**, use the Question and Answer section. Ideally you should attempt the questions yourself before reading the sample answers and examiner's comments and then compare your answer with the one given. If you do not have time for this, you should at least make brief plans that you could use as the basis of an answer to each question. Study the sample answer and the examiner's comments and then add the key points from them to your own answer or plan.

The examination

The Unit 3 examination lasts 1 hour and 30 minutes and there will be eight essay-style questions (one drawn from each of the eight topics) from which you must select and answer three. No section is compulsory, so you will have a free choice.

Each question is worth 25 marks overall, although some questions may be split into parts. You are guaranteed one question on each of the eight topics that comprise

Unit 3. To ensure that you can answer the question that has been set on a topic you must ensure you have studied and revised the entire subject content listed in the specification for that topic.

This paper will account for 50% of the total A2 marks and 25% of the total A-level.

Assessment objectives

In this psychology examination three sets of skills or assessment objectives are tested: AO1, AO2 and AO3.

AO1 (assessment objective 1) concerns questions designed to test your knowledge and understanding of psychological theories, terminology, concepts, studies and methods. You should be able to:
- recognise, recall and show understanding of knowledge
- select, organise and communicate relevant information in a variety of forms
- present and organise material clearly
- use relevant psychological terminology

AO2 (assessment objective 2) concerns questions designed to test your knowledge and understanding and the application of knowledge via analysis and evaluation of psychological theories, concepts, studies and methods. You should be able to:
- analyse and evaluate knowledge and processes
- apply knowledge and processes to novel situations, including those relating to issues
- assess the validity, reliability and credibility of information

AO3 (assessment objective 3) concerns questions designed to test your knowledge and application of knowledge and your understanding of how psychology as a science works. You should be able to:
- describe ethical, safe and skilful practical techniques and processes and the appropriate selection of qualitative and quantitative methods
- know how to make, record and communicate reliable and valid observations and measurements with appropriate accuracy and precision through using primary and secondary sources
- analyse, interpret, explain and evaluate the methodology, results and impact of experimental and investigative activities in a variety of ways

For each question there are 9 AO1 marks, 12 AO2 marks and 4 AO3 marks (a total of 75 possible marks on offer). You may sit this examination either in January or June of each year.

Good practice

For **AO1** you should:
- avoid 'story telling' or 'common sense' answers that lack psychological content
- give some depth to your answers and not just provide a list of points
- achieve a balance between the breadth and depth of your answer
- make your answer coherent; it should be clearly written and have a continuity to it so that it does not read as a series of unconnected comments

For **AO2/AO3** you should:
- elaborate upon evaluative points in order to construct an effective commentary
- where possible and appropriate, make use of both negative and positive criticism, for example methodological faults and practical applications
- draw conclusions and interpretations from your AO1 material
- select material carefully so that it is specifically directed at the question rather than just forming a general answer on the topic area
- avoid overuse of generic evaluation, such as the repetitive detailing of methodological strengths and weaknesses of the research studies included in your answer
- present arguments and evaluations with clarity
- ensure that you have included within your evaluation and analysis, material on relevant issues/debates/approaches, for example ethical issues and/or the nature–nurture debate

How the marks are awarded

Marks criteria for AO1 (5 marks)

5–4 marks	Outline is reasonably thorough, coherent and accurate.
3–2 marks	Outline is limited, reasonably coherent and generally accurate.
1 mark	Outline is weak and muddled.
0 marks	No creditworthy material is apparent.

Marks criteria for AO1

9–8 marks	**Sound** Knowledge and understanding are accurate and well detailed. A good range of relevant material has been presented. There is substantial evidence of breadth/depth. Organisation and structure of the answer are coherent.
7–5 marks	**Reasonable** Knowledge and understanding are generally accurate and reasonably detailed. A range of relevant material has been presented. There is evidence of breadth and/or depth. Organisation and structure of the answer are reasonably coherent.
4–3 marks	**Basic** Knowledge and understanding are basic/relatively superficial. A restricted range of material has been presented. Organisation and structure of the answer are basic.
2–1 marks	**Rudimentary** Knowledge and understanding are rudimentary and may be muddled and/or inaccurate. The material presented may be brief or largely irrelevant. The answer lacks organisation and structure.
0 marks	No creditworthy material is apparent.

Marks criteria for AO2/AO3

16–13 marks	**Effective** Evaluation shows sound analysis and understanding. Answer is well focused and displays coherent elaboration and/or a clear line of argument is apparent. Effective use of issues/debates/approaches. There is substantial evidence of synopticity. Well-structured ideas are expressed clearly and fluently. There is consistent effective use of psychological terminology and appropriate use of grammar, spelling and punctuation.
12–9 marks	**Reasonable** Evaluation shows reasonable analysis and evaluation. A generally focused answer that displays reasonable elaboration and/or line of argument is apparent. A reasonably effective use of issues/debates/approaches. There is evidence of synopticity. Most ideas are appropriately structured and expressed clearly. There is appropriate use of psychological terminology and there are some minor errors of grammar; spelling and punctuation only occasionally compromise meaning.
8–5 marks	**Basic** Evaluation and analysis show basic, superficial understanding. An answer that is sometimes focused and has some evidence of elaboration. There is a superficial use of issues/debates/approaches. There is some evidence of synopticity. The expression of ideas lacks clarity. There is limited use of psychological terminology and errors of grammar, spelling and punctuation are intrusive.
4–1 marks	**Rudimentary** Evaluation and analysis are rudimentary, showing very limited understanding. A weak, muddled and incomplete answer. Material is not used effectively and may be mainly irrelevant. Any reference to issues/debates/approaches is muddled or inaccurate. There is little or no evidence of synopticity. The expression of ideas is deficient, demonstrating confusion and ambiguity. The answer lacks structure and may be just a series of unconnected points. There are errors in grammar, spelling and punctuation that are frequent and intrusive.
0 marks	No creditworthy material is evident.

Explanation of examination injunctions

AO1

Outline: provide brief details without explanation

Describe: provide a detailed account without explanation

AO2

Evaluate: assess the value/effectiveness

Discuss: provide a reasoned, balanced account

Unit 3 topics

The Content Guidance section covers the main issues, themes and debates that you need to be familiar with in the study of the four A2 topics covered. The aim is to give an overview of these topics and to outline the key points you need to know in order to tackle the unit examination. However, it should be remembered that, for a full and adequate knowledge of the subject matter of this unit, you also need to study your textbook(s) and the notes you make during your course. You can use the points made in this section to organise your own notes and studies and as a revision aid when preparing for the examination.

Of the four topics covered in this guide the AQA specification requires you to study the following major areas:

- **Intelligence and learning**
  - Theories of intelligence
  - Animal learning and intelligence
  - Evolution of intelligence
- **Eating behaviour**
  - Eating behaviour
  - Biological explanations of eating behaviour
  - Eating disorders
- **Perception**
  - Theories of perceptual organisation
  - Development of perception
  - Face recognition and visual agnosias
- **Gender**
  - Psychological explanations of gender development
  - Biological influences on gender
  - Social contexts of gender role

Content Guidance

In this section, guidance is given on each of the three sub-sections of the four topics covered by this unit guide. Each sub-section starts by providing an outline and explanation of what the specification demands. This is then followed by a more detailed examination of the theories, research studies and evaluative points that each sub-section is made up of.

A general pattern for each topic is followed wherever appropriate, first providing an outline and explanation of what the specification demands. The subject matter is then described, research evidence given and finally further evaluative points made. It is important to remember that research evidence can be used as either descriptive material when answering examination questions (AO1) or as evaluation (AO2/AO3). It is advisable to learn how to make use of such material in an evaluative form, for instance by using wording such as 'this supports...' or 'this suggests...' etc. For the research quoted, names of researchers and publication dates have been given. Full references for these should be available in textbooks and via the internet if you desire to study them further.

Intelligence and learning

Theories of intelligence

Specification content

- *Theories of intelligence, including psychometric and information processing*
- *Gardner's theory of multiple intelligences*

There is a general requirement to have a knowledge of both psychometric and information processing theories. Specific theories are not named and so any theories of intelligence that fall into these categories would therefore be acceptable. However, Gardner's theory of multiple intelligences is specifically named and must therefore be included as part of your studies. An examination question might focus on one particular type of theory, such as psychometric theories, or specifically on Gardner's theory, or could ask for a comparison between theories.

Psychometric theories

Psychometrics is a scientific branch of psychology that seeks to quantify human qualities. Psychometric theories therefore perceive intelligence as being a set of abilities that are measurable by mental tests and there is a belief that intellectual differences between individuals can be determined. Psychometric theories differ in the number of basic factors that intelligence is considered to be made up of.

Spearman's (1904) two factor model

Spearman believed that there was a common factor that explained why individuals tend to score similarly on tests of different abilities. Using the statistical technique of **factor analysis** he identified two basic factors that intelligence tests measure.

- **General intelligence (g)** — a factor that underpins all mental abilities and is shared by individuals but in differing amounts.
- **Specific abilities (s)** — a factor that concerns specific skills that different individuals possess.

Spearman believed that all mental activities had both general and specific factors, but saw general intelligence as being more important as it showed intellectual differences between individuals. His theory became the starting point for the creation of other theories and for the justification for intelligence testing.

He saw general intelligence as being an innate quality and described it as a type of 'mental energy', it has even been suggested that (g) may relate to the efficiency of the nervous system.

Spearman saw his theory as being the gateway to psychology becoming an accepted scientific discipline.

Evaluation

- Spearman's work inspired focus and interest in the study of intelligence.
- His work led to the introduction of factor analysis into psychology, such as in the study of personality.
- Johnson and Bouchard (2005) using factor analysis to investigate the structure of mental ability, found a single, higher order factor of intelligence and concluded that general intelligence does indeed exist and contributes to all forms of intelligence.
- His theory was not widely accepted and multi-factor theories of intelligence became more popular.
- Kitcher (1985) states that there is no single measure of intellectual ability and that general intelligence is a myth.

Guildford's (1967) structure of intellect model

Guildford worked for the US air force and was trying to devise assessment criteria to select pilots. He was also motivated by his interest in creativity, rejecting the idea of a general intelligence factor. Unlike Spearman with his two-factor model, Guildford believed that there were 120 separate mental abilities. Using factor analysis Guildford proposed that intellectual abilities could be divided into five types of **operation** (type of thinking being used), four types of **content** (what is being thought about) and six kinds of **product** (type of answer required). He then set out to devise tests to measure each of the separate abilities.

Evaluation

- By 1985 Guildford had created tests to measure 70 separate mental abilities. However, scores achieved on these tests were often similar, suggesting they may be measuring the same ability and so there could be considerably less than 120 different mental abilities.
- The theory has proven practical applications in education. Structure of Intellect (SOI) is a teaching system based on Guildford's work that, by the identification of strengths and weaknesses, creates individual assessments and personalised learning programmes. SOI is currently used for children with learning difficulties and to enrich gifted individuals.
- Manning (1975) assessing SOI found it to be effective in helping gifted children to think more creatively.
- Bradfield and Slocumb (1997) also assessed SOI and found that it created better critical thinkers.
- Although intended as a general theory of intelligence, the structure of intellect model has other practical applications in personnel selection and placement. It has shown potential in career counselling and the development of foundational cognitive skills needed in the workplace. The program is also implemented in employment training programs and in business and industry.
- Psychometric theories stimulated a lot of interest and research into intelligence.
- Psychometric theories use factor analysis, producing objective statistical facts.

- Useful practical applications were created, such as IQ testing (although such tests have their opponents) and educational programmes.
- Duncan et al. (2000) have found biological support for the existence of (g). The use of PET scans while participants completed diverse intelligence tests showed that the lateral prefrontal cortex area of the brain was activated, but not when other non-intellectual activities were performed.
- If factor analysis is truly objective and scientific then intelligence should consist of an agreed number of factors. However, there are huge disagreements, ranging from Spearman's two factors to Guildford's 120.
- One methodological concern with factor analysis studies is that different researchers used different types of participants. Spearman used schoolchildren who have widely ranging intellects, while Guildford used college students who have a narrower range of intelligence. This may have contributed to finding different numbers of basic factors.
- Critics argue that psychometric theories do not explain anything about the mental processes involved in intelligence.
- The interpretation of factors produced by factor analysis can be criticised. Individual researchers decide which factors are independent and therefore data can be interpreted in a biased way that matches their beliefs about the fundamental nature of intelligence.

Information processing theories

Information processing theories present a cognitive approach and perceive intelligence as being dependent upon the stages a person goes through in order to create a solution to a problem. Intelligence is seen as constructed of a set of mental representations of information and the set of processes that acts upon them, such as paying attention and speed of processing. Attempts have been made to measure the speed of each step taken, with the assumption that these processes are performed in sequence (one after another). However, other researchers in the field believe that parallel processing may also be involved, where more than one process occurs at the same time.

Sternberg's (1977) triarchic theory of intelligence

Sternberg saw intelligence in terms of how well someone could cope with their environment, criticising psychometric theories for their narrow focus on measurable mental abilities and the identification of 'school smart' people. He was more interested in 'street smart' people, those who had the ability to adapt and shape their environment, but who did not perform well on IQ tests. His theory is regarded as the first cognitive theory and challenges the more established psychometric theories. Sternberg's theory is made up of three facets (sub-theories): **analytical**, **creative** and **practical**.

Analytical intelligence: similar to the psychometric viewpoint, a type of intelligence measured through academic problems and involving a series of three components, as listed in Table 1.

Table 1 Components of analytical intelligence

Type of component	Description
Metacomponents	Executive, higher-order control processes, involved in planning, problem solving and decision-making. Oversees *performance components* when carrying out desired actions
Performance components	Processes that undertake actions dictated by *metacomponents*. Uses long-term memory to permit perception of problems and relationships between objects and applies these relationships to decision-making and problem solving
Knowledge acquisition components	Processes used to acquire new knowledge. Selectively combines new information from diverse sources to complete tasks

Creative intelligence: deals with the relationship between intelligence and experience. Involves how well a task is performed in regard to a person's level of experience. Experience is seen as having two parts (see Table 2).

Table 2 Types of creative intelligence

Type of experience	Description
Novelty	Situations not experienced before. Gifted individuals can transfer skills from familiar experiences to unfamiliar (novel) experiences
Automation	Situations experienced many times before, therefore allowing other processes to be performed simultaneously (parallel processing)

Individuals may be gifted in one type of creative intelligence, but not necessarily both. Creative intelligence is also associated with **synthetic giftedness**, an ability to create new ideas and solve novel problems.

Practical intelligence: deals with the relationship between intelligence and an individual's external world. It involves the use of three processes to create a 'fit' between one's self and the environment (see Table 3).

Table 3 Process of practical intelligence

Type of process	Description
Adaptation	Involves a person changing within themselves in order to adjust to a changing environment
Shaping	Involves changing an environment to suit a person's needs
Selection	Involves choosing a new environment in preference to an existing inferior one to fit a person's needs

Practical intelligence is also associated with **practical giftedness**, an ability to apply new ideas and analytical skills to practical situations.

Evaluation

- Merrick (1992) used the Cognitive Abilities Self-Evaluative Questionnaire (CASE-Q) and found individuals with all three types of intelligence detailed by Sternberg, therefore supporting the components of his theory.
- Grigorenko et al. (2001) found that teaching methods based on Sternberg's theory that stressed analytical, creative and practical thinking were superior in improving reading ability than more conventional methods. This suggests that the theory has a positive practical application.
- Gottfredson (2003) believes that IQ tests do measure 'street smartness', in that they can predict a high scorers' ability to live longer, have a good job, stay out of jail etc.
- Gottfredson (2003) has also criticised the theory for its non-scientific nature, believing that Sternberg's component of practical intelligence is not a form of intelligence at all but merely task-specific knowledge; skills learned to cope with particular environments.

Case's (1985) information processing theory

Case was interested in how intelligence develops and was influenced by Piaget's theory of cognitive development. The theory describes how information processing ability is related to the degree of **M-space** (mental capacity) a person possesses.

Information processing ability is seen as developing over time due to three factors, as listed in Table 4.

Table 4 Three factors of information processing ability

Type of factor	Description
Brain maturity	The conductivity of the myelin sheath grows with age, leading to nerve signals transmitting faster
Cognitive strategies	Processing capacity increases as the degree of M-space needed to process mastered skills decreases
Metacognitive skills	Mental skills crucial to efficient use of M-space. A set of mental operations are used to change a 'problem situation' into a 'solution situation'

Evaluation

- Case's theory explains the qualitative changes in the development of intelligence.
- The Neuhaus Education Centre (2008) found that it was possible to increase metacognitive skills by teaching students to use word webs. Spelling ability and vocabulary usage improved, suggesting a practical application to the theory.
- The theory can be seen in objective, scientific terms as it sees intelligence as measurable due to the capacity of M-space being determinable.
- Chi (1978) found that child chess players who used metacognitive skills could recall more positions on a board than adults who did not have the same skills. This lends support to Case's theory.

- Information processing theories tend to have practical applications, especially in education.
- Psychometric theories merely describe intelligence, whereas information processing theories explain how problems are solved by identifying the cognitive processes involved.
- Information processing theories identify a much broader scope of abilities than the narrow focus of psychometric theories.

Gardner's theory (1983) of multiple intelligences

Gardner saw all individuals as possessing a **cognitive profile** involving different amounts of various kinds of intelligence. The theory is basically an educational theory, as Gardner believes schools should be offering individual teaching programmes that fit each person's cognitive profile and improve their intellectual weaknesses.

Gardner also thought that there was a danger, by not acknowledging certain types of intelligence, of undervaluing individuals who possessed high levels of ability in those areas. Each person's cognitive profile was seen as being based upon eight core types of intelligence (see Table 5).

Table 5 Eight core types of intelligence

Type of intelligence	Description
Bodily-kinaesthetic	Concerns bodily movements. Learning occurs by physical interaction, e.g. sports players.
Interpersonal	Concerns interactions with others. Learning occurs through group discussion, e.g. managers.
Intrapersonal	Concerns self-awareness. Learning occurs via introspection, e.g. scientists.
Linguistic	Concerns the use of language. Learning occurs by reading and note-making, e.g. writers.
Logical-mathematical	Concerns logic. Learning occurs by reasoning and the use of numbers, e.g. engineers.
Musical	Concerns sensitivity to sound and music. Learning occurs by auditory means, e.g. musicians.
Naturalistic	Concerns the natural world. Learning occurs by sensitivity to nature, e.g. farmers.
Spatial	Concerns vision and spatial judgement. Learning occurs by visualisation and mental manipulation, e.g. architects.

Several criteria were used to provide evidence for the existence of each type of intelligence, for instance, being talented in one type but not another and neurological evidence indicating specialised brain areas and unique developmental trends.

Other types of multiple intelligences have been suggested, such as **existential** (philosophical) and **moral** intelligence.

Evaluation

- Musical and bodily-kinaesthetic intelligences have been criticised as being talents rather than types of intelligence.
- As no current tests exist that can identify and measure Gardner's intelligence types, they have been accused of being merely personality types rather than distinct forms of intelligence.
- Naturalistic intelligence has been criticised as being more of an interest than a type of intelligence. However, it may be a form of intelligence for cultures where people live closer to nature.
- Kornhaber (2001) believes the theory matches what teachers' experience, in that people think and learn in a wide variety of ways. This has led to the theory being incorporated successfully into many teaching practices, allowing the development of new methods to meet the range of learning styles students possess.
- Turner (2008) provided evidence for the existence of a separate musical intelligence. Teachers used memorable tunes to successfully fit in lyrics representing material being learned.
- Traub (1999) reported on evidence from neuroscience supporting the idea of each intelligence type having localised function in the brain. Brain imaging and studies of brain-damaged individuals showed different mental activities to be associated with different brain areas, lending support to the theory.
- Marchand (2008) found evidence supporting the idea of a separate bodily-kinaesthetic intelligence. Mud masons in Mali communicated building skills without using words, but by physical repetition. This could have a practical application in teaching apprentices.

Animal learning and intelligence

Specification content

- *Nature of simple learning (classical and operant conditioning) and its role in the behaviour of non-human animals*
- *Evidence for intelligence in non-human animals, for example self-recognition, social learning, Machiavellian intelligence*

The focus is on simple forms of animal learning and how these learning types affect behaviour. Classical and operant conditioning are specifically named and so must be studied. There is also a direct requirement to have a knowledge and understanding of evidence for intelligence in non-human animals. Note that the specification entry states 'for example'. This means that there is no direct requirement to study the specific examples given, nor would there ever be a specific requirement to address them in an examination question. The examples are just there for guidance, meaning that they are advisable areas to cover in the study of this topic.

Nature of simple learning (classical and operant conditioning)

Classical and operant conditioning are from the behaviourist tradition, which sees learning occurring as a result of experience via the process of association. In classical conditioning a **stimulus** becomes associated with a **response**, while operant conditioning involves learning behaviour due to its consequences. Classical conditioning is associated with behaviour not under conscious control, while operant conditioning is associated with voluntary behaviour.

Classical conditioning

Pavlov (1927) researching into the salivation reflex of dogs, noticed that the dogs salivated before food was presented as they were able to predict its arrival due to other environmental features becoming associated with their feeding, for example the sight of a food bowl. Therefore the dogs had learned to produce a natural reflex (salivation) to a stimulus not normally associated with that response. Pavlov then found that by pairing the presentation of food with the sound of a bell, he could quickly get the dogs to salivate to the sound of the bell alone. This process is detailed in the box below.

Before learning: food (unconditioned stimulus) → salivation (unconditioned response)

During learning: food (UCS) + bell (neutral stimulus) → salivation (UCR)

After learning: bell (conditioned stimulus) → salivation (conditioned response)

In a subsequent series of experiments various features of classical conditioning were illustrated as described in Table 6.

Table 6 Features of classical conditioning

Type of feature	Description of feature
One-trial learning	A form of classical conditioning where just one pairing of a UCS and a CS produces a CR.
First and second order conditioning	First order conditioning involves pairing a CS with a UCS that directly satisfies a biological urge, while with second order conditioning the CS is paired with a UCS that only indirectly satisfies the biological urge.
Generalisation	The conditioning process can be generalised by slightly varying the CS to produce weaker forms of the CR.
Discrimination	Discrimination occurs when the UCS is paired with one specific CS and the CR occurs to this pairing only.
Extinction	If the CS is continually given without the presentation of the UCS, the CR grows weaker and then ceases.
Spontaneous recovery	After apparent extinction, if a rest period is given followed by re-presentation of the CS, the CR is revived.

Operant conditioning

Operant conditioning is based upon Thorndike's (1911) **law of effect**, which states that behaviours resulting in pleasant outcomes are likely to be repeated in similar circumstances, while behaviours resulting in unpleasant outcomes are unlikely to be repeated.

Under controlled laboratory conditions Skinner (1938) built upon Thorndike's work, using a **Skinner box** where animals would be rewarded with food pellets for producing desired behaviours. An animal would accidentally produce a behaviour, such as pressing a lever causing a food pellet to be released. Gradually the animal would learn to associate this behaviour with the reward and thus produce the behaviour every time. The food pellet (or any form of reward) is known as a **reinforcement** because it strengthens the chances of the behaviour occurring again.

There are four possible outcomes of any behaviour:
- **Positive reinforcement** — receiving something pleasant, e.g. food.
- **Negative reinforcement** — not receiving something unpleasant, e.g. not having to do chores.
- **Positive punishment** — receiving something unpleasant, e.g. being grounded.
- **Negative punishment** — not receiving something pleasant, e.g. not being given a promised treat.

Reinforcements increase the chances of a behaviour recurring, while punishments decrease the chances.

Reinforcements can be **primary**, where they occur naturally and directly satisfy biological needs, e.g. food; or **secondary**, where they have to be learned and therefore indirectly satisfy biological needs, e.g. money.

Behaviour shaping: a method of achieving target behaviour by reinforcing behaviours that gradually resemble the desired outcome.

Reinforcement schedules: by varying the frequency at which reinforcements are given affects the rate at which an animal will respond.

Role of learning in non-human animals

Animals have been shown to use conditioning to learn about their environment and adapt to changing environments. Research in both laboratory and natural settings has shown that classical conditioning is used by animals to learn whether food sources are safe or not. However, **biological preparedness**, where the tendency to learn associations is dependent on biological predispositions to do so, also plays a role.

Operant conditioning allows animals to interact with their environment and then, by the process of **trial and error learning**, shape their behaviour via reinforcement and punishment processes, e.g. to find food and avoid danger.

Research

- Garcia and Koelling (1966) showed how laboratory rats learn taste aversions by classical conditioning. The rats were exposed to radiation but came to associate the sickness they felt with the taste of their plastic feeding bottle and refused to drink from it.
- Garcia et al. (1990) showed that taste aversions also occur naturally, as coyotes fed mutton laced with poison refused to approach live sheep.
- Sahley et al. (1981) showed that one-trial learning occurs in animals. Slugs, exposed just once to an attractive food odour mixed with a bitter taste, displayed a reduced preference for that food odour.
- Garcia and Koelling (1966) showed that rats learn to not drink a sweet liquid paired with an injection that makes them sick, a natural behaviour. However, if the liquid was paired with an electric shock, the rats continue to drink as rats do not have a natural tendency to avoid things linked to electric shocks. This links to Seligman's (1970) idea of biological preparedness (see description above).
- Baker (1984) showed that pigeons use trial and error learning to discover how to use landmarks as navigational aids.
- Fisher and Hinde (1949) showed that animals tend to learn behaviours that resemble innate ones. Blue tits seemingly learned by imitation to drink cream from milk bottles, but this artificial behaviour was easily learned as it resembled their natural behaviour of stripping tree bark.
- Guildford (2004) showed that although pigeons have been seen to navigate by flying above motorways, this may be because it resembles their innate ability to navigate using rivers and coastlines.
- Breland and Breland (1961) demonstrated instinctive drift, where animals revert to natural behaviours. Pigs trained to put tokens in a piggy bank to get rewards preferred instead to root in the ground with them.

Evaluation

- Although classical conditioning cannot explain how new behaviours arise, operant conditioning, by the use of reinforcement, can and thus complex behaviours too.
- In addition to classical and operant conditioning, animals also use social learning via observation and imitation.
- Behaviourism does not account for innate influences, e.g. biological preparedness and instinctive drift.
- Behaviourism sees behaviour as being determined by the environment and therefore sees no role for free will.
- Some uses of conditioning may be unethical, like training animals for warfare.
- Behaviourism does not account for the role of emotional and cognitive factors in determining behaviour. Kohler (1925) suggested chimpanzees use insight learning, where novel thinking is used to solve a problem.
- Operant conditioning cannot explain latent learning, where learning seemingly occurs without reinforcement. Tolman (1930) showed that rats learned to navigate

a maze without being rewarded, but only demonstrated this learning when given the incentive of a reward.

Evidence for intelligence in non-human animals

Intelligence in animals can be seen as a hierarchy of learning processes, with species differing in the degree of behaviour that is learned. Alternatively intelligence in animals can be seen as their ability to learn and process information. Ultimately animal intelligence is closely associated with the capacity to survive and successfully breed. Research has concentrated on **social learning**, **self-recognition** and **Machiavellian intelligence**.

Social learning

Social learning refers to behavioural processes affecting what animals learn via social interactions. It involves the copying of behaviour and several forms have been identified that concentrate on the ability to solve social problems.

- **Imitation**: behaviour is observed and then directly copied.
- **Enhancement**: attention is directed to a particular feature of the environment in order to solve a problem.
- **Emulation**: the consequences of a behaviour are reproduced.
- **Tutoring**: a model encourages, punishes or provides behavioural examples to enable others to acquire skills, usually at a cost to the model.

Imitation, enhancement and **emulation** are all passive forms, as the model does not deliberately set out to be copied. **Tutoring** is an active form, where the model does.

Research

- Whiten (1999) found that in chimpanzee colonies different population-specific behaviours arose in using twigs to eat ants, suggesting that such behaviours are learned by individuals directly imitating each other.
- Kawai (1965) showed how snow monkeys apparently imitated a monkey who washed potatoes before eating them. However, Nagell (1993) suggests that this was due to attention being focused onto the potatoes and the water, enhancing the chances of the skill being learned by trial and error.
- Tomasello et al. (1987) reported on chimpanzees that emulated a model that demonstrated using a rake to get food. The chimpanzees did not imitate the model's particular actions but developed their own technique, suggesting they were trying to attain the consequences of the behaviour.
- Rendell and Whitehead (2001) reported that adult orcas act as tutors by delaying the killing and eating of prey, so that youngsters may practice their hunting skills.

Evaluation

- There are few examples of tutoring and these are disputed. Adult orcas may not be delaying killing in order for youngsters to learn, they may simply be playing with their food.

- Due to subjective interpretation it is not always clear how a behaviour has arisen, for instance via imitation or enhancement.
- Dugatkin (2000) believes social learning is crucial in order to avoid predators (demonstrated by blackbirds and monkeys) and maximise mate selection (shown by guppies and quail). However, this is a recent claim and needs more evidence.
- Social learning may show the origins of culture; chimpanzees show population-specific behaviours, a demonstration of culture in human terms. However, Galef (1992) says this can only be true if animals transmit behaviours across generations by direct learning involving imitation and tutoring. Tutoring by animals lacks convincing evidence and true imitation is rarely found.

Self-recognition

Self-recognition is associated with possession of a self-concept, seen as necessary for higher levels of intelligence. Most research has involved the mirror-test, whereby an animal has a dot painted on its head while anaesthetised. The degree of dot touching, with and without a mirror, is then recorded. All species of great apes as well as elephants, dolphins and orcas have demonstrated this ability. More recently less expected species have also shown this talent, which has created heated debate.

Research

- Gallup (1977) found that chimpanzees and orang-utans are able to self-recognise using his mirror test.
- Epstein et al. (1981) used the mirror test and reported the surprising finding that pigeons demonstrated self-recognition.
- Prior et al. (2008) marked magpies with either a bright colour or a non-noticeable 'sham' colour, or not at all. Mark-directed behaviour only occurred when brightly marked and in the presence of a mirror, suggesting that magpies can self-recognise.

Evaluation

- The fact that species such as pigeons seem to self-recognise cast doubts on whether the mirror-test is a valid measurement of the ability. Pigeons are not generally a species credited with higher cognitive skills.
- Some bird species, such as magpies, need a high degree of intelligence as they must recognise and recall which other species members observed them storing food in order to prevent stealing. Therefore some bird species may be capable of self-recognition.
- The mirror-test may not be suitable for many species as a test of self-recognition, e.g. species that mainly use senses other than sight. This suggests that it cannot be seen as a valid measure of self-awareness.
- The ability to self-recognise in mirrors is not universally accepted as demonstrating self-awareness. Nefian and Hayes (1998) see it instead as evidence of a body concept, where an animal has learned to differentiate between itself and external stimuli.

Machiavellian intelligence

Machiavellian intelligence perceives the demands of the social world as being the main determinant of intelligence. Intelligent individuals look after their own interests, often by using deception or forming coalitions, but without disturbing social cohesion.

Research

- Whiten and Byrne (1988) showed how young baboons use deceit to get their mothers to chase adults away from foodstuffs so that they may eat them.
- Maestripieri (2007) showed how female macaques use Machiavellian intelligence by having sex with a dominant male so he will protect a new born infant, while having sex without his knowledge with other males, so that they will provide similar protection if the dominant male dies.
- Nishida et al. (1992) reported that alpha males do not share food with rivals but do with non-rivals so they will assist in any power struggles.
- Kummer (1967) showed that female Hamadryas baboons successfully threaten rivals by sitting in front of the harem male so that any threat is seen as directed at him.

Evaluation

- There is strong evidence that Machiavellian intelligence exists in primates, especially those living in large social groups with high social complexity and an ability to memorise socially relevant information.
- The evolution of advanced cognitive abilities necessary for Machiavellian intelligence has not been adequately explained as yet.
- Some examples of Machiavellian intelligence might be explained as conditioned responses that occurred through experience via reinforcement and which are then exhibited again in similar circumstances.

Evolution of intelligence

Specification content

- Evolutionary factors in the development of human intelligence, for example ecological demands, social complexity, brain size
- Role of genetic and environmental factors associated with intelligence test performance, including the influence of culture

The focus is on the evolutionary approach, so this part of the specification is useful as its general themes can be applied to other areas that involve evolutionary theory. The focus initially is on evolutionary factors that affect the development of intelligence in humans, but note again that the specification entry states 'for example'. This means that there is no direct requirement to study the specific examples given, nor would there ever be a specific requirement to address them in an examination question. The examples are just there for guidance, meaning that they are advisable areas to cover. There is also a need to have a knowledge and understanding of genetic and environmental factors that may influence performance on tests of intelligence. As the influence of culture is specifically identified this particular area must be studied and may directly occur in the wording of an examination question.

Evolutionary factors in the development of human intelligence

The evolutionary approach believes that human intelligence evolved due to the demands of an ever-changing environment creating selective pressure for increased intellect. There was a need to contend with the ecological challenges of foraging for food, deal with increasing social complexity and develop a more advanced brain.

Ecological demands

Intelligence is perceived as being able to thrive in a given environment, especially by having good foraging abilities. Humans were able to adapt to global cooling in paleothic times by finding food and exploiting new environments due to the development of higher mental skills, such as co-operative hunting and tool use. As plants are only periodically available hunting meat became a necessity. Being a good forager required intelligence, which would have increased survival and led to the ability being naturally selected.

Foraging hypotheses
- Milton (1988) hypothesised that increased intellect is due to the demands of foraging. Developing mental maps would help fruit-eaters to know when and where to look for food and they would develop this ability by monitoring the availability of different fruits.
- Gibson (1987) proposed the **food extraction hypothesis**, seeing the need to find hidden foods as having driven the evolution of intelligence. Cognitive processing, manual dexterity and tool use would have been necessary and created selective pressure for a larger cortex.

Research
- Dunbar (1992) tested Milton's hypothesis, examining the amount of fruit in an animal's diet and the size of its neocortex. No significant relationship was found, therefore not supporting the idea. However, only small amounts of fruit may be needed to supply necessary nutrition, casting doubts on Dunbar's conclusion.
- Boesche et al. (1992) tested Gibson's hypothesis and found that chimpanzees' use of tools to open nuts closely matched archaeological evidence of early nomadic humans noted for their foraging skills. This supports the hypothesis.

Evaluation

- Fruit is often difficult to locate but more nutritious than abundant leaves. Fruit-eaters tend to have larger brains than leaf-eaters, supporting the idea that the demands of foraging led to increased intelligence. However, Dunbar's findings cast doubt on this, see research.

- Many animal species have cognitive maps for stored food items, therefore it seems unlikely that developing mental maps produces cognitive evolution.
- Milton's foraging hypothesis does not explain why fruit-eaters need a high quality diet. Did they need more energy to fuel a larger brain, or did their brains grow to develop the skills to find fruit?
- With the food extraction hypothesis the levels of difficulty in extracting foodstuffs are not well explained, meaning the hypothesis is difficult to test.
- It is not clear if extractive foraging is a cause or an effect of intelligence. However, Parker and Gibson (1979) believe that animals that extract one food type all the time tend to use tools in an unintelligent way, while those who extract many types display more intelligent tool use. Therefore they see tool use as a consequence of intelligence.
- Foraging skills may involve different brain areas. Monitoring food supplies and extraction skills are seen as involving the neocortex, while the hippocampus, prefrontal and parietal lobes have been associated with the construction of mental maps.

Social complexity

Social living has advantages, but conflicts arise. Intelligent individuals are ones who can solve such problems.

The social complexity hypothesis

This hypothesis sees intelligence as being social in nature and developing due to the need to anticipate, respond to and manipulate group members. There is a need to understand the mental world of others and to have Machiavellian intelligence to interact with and manipulate others. Advanced abilities in social cognition should be evident in those living in large, complex groups and such animals should possess a large frontal cortex.

Research

- Holekamp and Engh (2003) found a strong positive correlation between brain size and complexity of social living in carnivores, supporting the hypothesis.
- Holekamp and Engh (2004) found that hyenas living in complex groups had advanced social cognition abilities, recognising dominance rankings between individuals in encounters in which they were not directly involved. This also supports the hypothesis.
- Ehmer et al. (2001) found larger brain structures in female paper wasps that live in social colonies than solitary females, again supporting the hypothesis.
- Bond (2003) tested pinyon jays, which are highly social and western jays, which are not, on their abilities to memorise pairs of ranked objects. The pinyon jays were superior, suggesting that social complexity and higher intelligence are linked.

Evaluation

- The predictions of the social complexity hypothesis of advanced social cognition abilities and larger brain structures are supported by research.

- Evidence from observations of animals often involves subjective interpretation that may be subject to researcher bias.
- An important ethical issue concerns care being taken when performing studies on wild animals to not lower their fitness in any way.
- Evidence shows that neocortical increases occur as group size increases, lending support to the social complexity hypothesis.
- Evolutionary explanations have been accused of being reductionist as they reduce complex behaviours down to one explanation of adaptiveness. They are also deterministic in that they see behaviour as caused by past environments with no role for free will.

Brain size

The evolution of increased brain size has been associated with the need for body coordination and to cope with group living, Machiavellian intelligence and ecological demands.

Big brains are costly and do not ensure high intelligence. Comparing brain size to body weight is also problematic.

The **encephalisation quotient (EQ)** comprises brain mass of a species divided by expected brain size for body size. Humans score highest, but some species outscore seemingly more intelligent ones. Humans possess the largest number of cortical neurons, although not enough to explain cognitive differences with other species.

The best measure of brain capacity is regarded as the number of cortical neurons combined with the conductive speed of cortical fibres, which reflects the speed of information processing. Humans are dominant.

Research
- Lynn (1989) showed that brain size has increased in humans threefold, suggesting large brains bring increased intelligence, although human brains have no specific characteristic indicating cleverness.
- Willerman et al. (1991) did a meta-analysis of the relationship between brain volume and IQ. A positive correlation was found, suggesting brain size and intelligence are related.
- Narr et al. (2006) investigated the relationship between cortical thickness and IQ. A positive correlation was found, again suggesting brain size is related to intelligence.
- Sassaman and Zartler (1982) studied children with abnormally small brains, 40% were not retarded, suggesting brain size may not reflect intelligence.

Evaluation
- Studies that use IQ scores may be flawed as IQ may only measure one aspect of intelligence.
- Crows have shown astonishing intelligent tool use, planning and cognitive flexibility, but have small brains compared to other birds. However, they have a relatively large cortex, which may be the source of their intelligence.

- Humphrey (1999) believes that if big brains are not related to general intelligence, they must contribute to other evolutionary specialisms such as language abilities.

Role of genetic and environmental factors associated with intelligence test performance

IQ tests claim (controversially) to measure intelligence. Twin and adoption studies have been conducted and if differences in IQ are mainly genetic then people with close genetic relationships should have similar IQ scores. If intelligence is genetic, then IQ levels should not be affected by experience and therefore attempts to increase IQ by enrichment should not work. Recently attempts have been made to identify specific genes, but more research is needed. Findings from these various studies have not drawn clear conclusions and have attracted heated debate. The effect of cultural influences on IQ has proven controversial, especially attempts to create culture-free tests.

Genetic factors

Twin studies

These studies examine the relationship between genetic similarity in people and their IQ scores. If the correlation is high, it is taken as evidence supporting the genetic argument.

Research

- Bouchard and McGue (1981) performed a meta-analysis that showed MZ (identical and 100% genetically similar) twins had a concordance rate of 0.86, much higher than less related individuals. However, MZ twins raised together often have identical environments.
- Shields (1962) found that MZ twins reared apart had a concordance rate of 0.77, similar to MZ twins reared together, 0.76, while for DZ twins (50% genetically similar) reared together, the concordance rate was only 0.51, suggesting that intelligence is largely genetic. Similar findings were found by other researchers. However, such studies have their criticisms, see evaluation.
- Thompson et al. (2000) found that MZ twins had more similar brain structures than DZ twins in areas associated with intelligence when MRI brain scans were conducted, suggesting that intelligence is genetic in nature.

> **Evaluation**
>
> - 'Separated twins' often had similar environments, e.g. raised by similar families. In the Shield's study, separated MZ twins raised in dissimilar families only had a concordance rate of 0.51, which throws doubt onto the genetic argument.
> - An influential researcher, Cyril Burt, who favoured the view that intelligence is inherited, was found to have fabricated his results, which weakens the genetic argument.
> - There is debate over how identical some twins actually are and how similar shared environments were. This makes analysis of results difficult.
> - If intelligence was entirely genetic then concordance rates for MZ twins would be 100%. As they are not, environment must play a role, indeed all genes need an environment in which to express themselves.

Adoption studies

If intelligence is genetic then adopted children should have IQ scores closer to their biological parents than their adopted ones.

Research

- Horne (1983) found that adopted children are closer to their biological mothers on IQ scores. Adopted children with high-IQ biological mothers outperformed adopted children with low-IQ biological mothers when raised in similar intellectual environments. These findings support the genetic argument.
- Petrill and Deater-Deckard (2004) looked at families containing biological and adopted children. Mothers were closer in IQ terms to biological than adopted children. However, IQ performance was also related to age when adopted and time spent in the adoptive home, suggesting that environment also plays a role.

Evaluation

- Just like twin studies, adoption studies do not allow clear conclusions to be made.
- The environment of the adoptive home can often not be that different to the biological home, making research inferences difficult.
- Important factors are often not controlled and IQ scores of biological parents difficult to confirm.

Gene identification

Attempts have been made to identify specific genes involved in the inheritance of intelligence. Individual genes may only have slight influences, but collectively exert great influence.

Research

- Plomin et al. (1998) found that a variant of the I.G.F.2 receptor gene was common among high-IQ children, although the gene only accounts for about four IQ points and only half the children had it.
- Lahn et al. (2004) identified a gene, ASPM, linked to higher intelligence. ASPM appears to have affected the expansion of the cerebral cortex, which may explain how genes influence intelligence.

Evaluation

- Gene identification could help us to not only understand intelligence but also learning disabilities and intellectual decay, which may lead to effective therapies.
- Kihlstrom (1998) fears research may be abused and centres that test for intelligent genes and attempt selective breeding or abort 'non-intelligent' pregnancies may be established.
- People may misunderstand the research and mistakenly believe that genes alone determine intelligence.

Environmental factors

Family influences

IQ may be affected by how much social stimulation occurs.

Research

- Saltz (1973) found that children in institutional care, paired with a foster-grandparent, improved their IQ, suggesting social stimulation aids intellectual development.
- Zajonc and Markus (1975) found that as families grow in size less stimulation is given to later children and their IQ is lower. However, the effect was small.

Evaluation

- The research suggests a practical application to raise impoverished children's IQ levels.
- Research implies that the fall in American IQ levels may be due to the trend for larger families and the reduced social stimulation that then occurs.

Enrichment

If intelligence is genetic then enrichment should not increase IQ.

Research

- Atkinson (1990) reviewed several enrichment programmes and found parental involvement, leading to stimulation at home, raised IQ levels and social skills.
- Heber (1972) reported on the Milwaukee project. Enriched children had vastly improved IQ levels. However, scores later declined although poor subsequent schooling may have been to blame.

Evaluation

- In general, enrichment programmes seem able to boost intellectual performance, especially in the short term.
- Parental involvement appears to be a key factor in boosting children's confidence and motivation to do well.
- Evidence indicates that improved diet and intellectual enrichment play a part.

Influence of culture

IQ tests are biased in favour of the culture they represent, testing the skills and knowledge of that culture. Attempts have been made to create **culture-free tests** where questions are not culturally based and allow fair comparison of everyone. Poverty is another cultural factor, with minority cultural groups often living in impoverished conditions, which can have an effect on IQ levels.

Research

- Williams (1972) devised the Black Intelligence Test for Cultural Homogeneity (BITCH) based on black culture. Black people, who score poorly on traditional white-cultural tests, did well, while white people scored poorly, suggesting that IQ tests are culturally biased.
- Brooks-Gunn et al. (1996) reviewing longitudinal data on black and white children, found poverty accounted for over 50% of the difference in IQ, indicating poverty to be an important cultural factor influencing IQ.

- Culture-free tests are culturally biased as testing itself is a cultural concept.
- Vernon (1969) says that intelligence is different things in different cultures and not something we all share in differing amounts measurable by IQ tests.
- Research into cultural influences is socially sensitive, raising a range of ethical concerns.

Eating behaviour

Specification content

- *Factors influencing attitudes to food and eating behaviour, for example cultural influences, mood, health concerns*
- *Explanations for the success or failure of dieting*

The factors that the specification lists as influencing food and eating behaviour are merely examples with no specific requirement to study them, neither will they feature directly in any examination question. It would be perfectly acceptable to include material on other relevant factors in examination answers, but it is advisable to study the examples given, as they would provide an appropriate and detailed source of material.

Explanations for the success and failure of dieting are wide ranging and can be drawn from most psychological approaches and there is a wide range of research evidence to draw on. The key element is to use material studied in a manner that directly addresses examination questions. You may be asked to outline explanations and/or evaluate them.

Factors influencing attitudes to food and eating behaviour

Eating is necessary to survival. Many factors influence attitudes to food and eating, with the three prime ones being mood, cultural influences and health concerns. Sensory qualities have an influence too, either through learning or an innate basis. Information about food helps to form expectations and therefore affects behaviour and our social environment can also directly or indirectly have an influence. Individual differences are a mediating factor too.

Mood
Emotional states can affect eating practices, either in small ways, or in ways that can help to explain abnormal eating practices, such as binge eating.

Research
- Wansink et al. (2008) offered popcorn and grapes to participants and found that people watching a sad film ate more popcorn to try and cheer themselves up, while those watching a comedy ate more grapes to try and prolong their mood.

- Wolff et al. (2000) found that female binge eaters had more negative moods on binge-eating days than female normal eaters, suggesting that negative moods are related to abnormal eating practices.

Cultural influences

Different cultural and sub-cultural groups have different eating practices that are transmitted to group members, usually via reinforcement and social learning. Cultural attitudes to the health concerns of food and eating also vary widely. Culture influences behaviour directly, but more usually has a moderating role on other variables to determine individual eating practices.

Research

- Stefansson (1960) reported on the isolated Copper Eskimos who lived on flesh and roots. When given sugar it disgusted them, suggesting that sweet tastes are not necessarily universal to all cultures.
- McFarlane and Pliner (1987) found that only sub-cultural groups who consider nutrition to be important prefer healthy food. But this is mediated by socio-economic factors, if healthy food is expensive, low-income groups will not eat healthily.

Health concerns

The desire to eat nutritious food and avoid an unhealthy diet can affect attitudes and behaviour. There are differences between individuals and cultural groupings.

Research

- Monneuse et al. (1991) found people with a preference for high sugar content in dairy products actually chose items with lower sugar content, suggesting that health concerns do affect eating behaviour.
- Tuorila and Pangborn (1988) found that women had intentions to eat healthily, but that actual consumption of dairy products and high-fat foods was based more on sensory qualities of food, showing that attitudes do not necessarily reflect behaviour.
- Steptoe et al. (1995) ranked factors taken into account when selecting food. Sensory qualities were ranked highest, above health concerns, indicating that healthy eating is not the most important factor in determining behaviour.

Other factors

Several other factors have a mediating effect on food related attitudes and behaviour.

Sensory qualities: the shape, smell, taste, etc. of food can have an influence on whether it is eaten.

- Hetherington and Rolls (1996) found that if sensory qualities of a food are perceived negatively, it will not be eaten.
- Cowart (1981) found innate liking of sweet foods and dislike of bitter and sour foods. This may be linked to survival, showing which foods are safe.
- Bartoshuk (1994) found that attractive food smells are learned, indicating a role for nurture.

Social environment: eating rate, style and amount can be affected by one's social environment either directly, e.g. by the presence of others, or indirectly, e.g. by local culinary traditions.

- De Castro (1991) found a **social facilitation effect**, in that the presence of others made people eat more.

Personality: different personalities are attracted, or not, to different types of food and eating behaviour.

- Stone and Pangborn (1990) reported that sensation-seeking personalities are drawn towards stimulating and hazardous eating behaviours and neophobics (people who fear anything unknown) are reluctant to eat novel foodstuffs.

Information: a strong mediating factor on eating behaviour, especially relating to health concerns, is the effect that information can have.

- Martins et al. (1997) found that information on the health qualities of food has positive, negative or neutral effects. These effects are dependent upon the types of food being portrayed, the way the information is presented and individual attitudes and expectations towards foods.
- Engell et al. (1998) found that people with a higher concern for being healthy are more influenced by information concerning nutrition, suggesting people's attitudes towards the health consequences of certain foods is a moderating factor between information given and actual behaviour.

Evaluation

- Research on mood states suggests that comfort foods should display nutritional information to stop depressed people eating badly, such habits can contribute to becoming bulimic.
- Eating behaviour can be seen as an inter-relation of internal variables, such as sensory qualities and external variables, such as social context. This suggests that it is the influence of several factors mediating upon each other that ultimately determines attitudes and behaviour, rather than single factors alone.
- The findings from research studies could be used to create eating programmes that shape and maintain healthy dietary practices, for instance in the way that information about healthy eating is presented and which groups are targeted.
- For a fuller understanding of the topic area both nurture and nature need to be considered, i.e. the effects of learning experiences and innate food preferences.

Explanations for the success or failure of dieting

Dieting is a form of restrained eating involving voluntary restriction of food intake. Dieting is not a modern behaviour. The ability to diet bestowed an adaptive value in times of food shortages. There is a strong need for successful forms of dieting as obesity has become epidemic. Bartlett (2003) reports that in America over 50% of people are obese or overweight and 300,000 deaths a year are credited to preventable weight-related conditions.

Wing and Hill (2001) defined success as, 'successful long-term weight loss maintenance, involving the intentional loss of at least 10% of initial body weight and keeping it off for at least one year'. According to this definition 20% succeed.

There are several explanations for the success and failure of dieting, involving a range of biological and psychological factors. However, these should generally be considered in conjunction with each other (multi-causal), rather than as individual explanations. Dieters differ in the extent to which eating is restrained and for how long and these factors also affect success levels.

Explanations for success

Success is often related to being taught skills useful for weight maintenance, rather than just how to lose weight. **Relapse prevention** is a means of achieving a stable energy balance around a lower weight. It involves teaching the identification of situations in which 'lapses' may occur and how to 're-focus' if they do occur, in order that there is no return to pre-weight loss eating behaviours.

Motivation is a prime factor in determining success; financial incentives and social support have been focused upon. Financial incentives are intended as a form of **positive reinforcement** creating, by operant conditioning, the desired weight-loss effect. The use of social networks can be beneficial by teaching spouses and significant others to provide support during the weight-loss time period. **Weight watchers** is a dieting organisation that encourages members to provide support for each other. Successful role models are also provided and a positive social identity is created for individual members, motivating them to succeed.

Goal-setting is another motivational factor that can increase the chances of dieting success. This is dependent on setting achievable targets for the amount of weight loss and the time period in which it is to occur. Maximising chances of success is best achieved by not setting over-specific goals and the goal-setting process should consist of a series of short-term goals leading up to the ultimate long-term goal. Initial targets are easy to achieve, increasing confidence and motivation. Regular monitoring and feedback occur, with necessary re-adjustments being made. Expert opinions are sought, but individuals are involved in target setting to create a sense of 'ownership'.

People who have successfully dieted tend to share common behaviours that promote weight loss and its maintenance (see research). Once weight loss has been maintained for 2 years, the chances of long-term success increase dramatically.

Research

- Thomas and Stern (1995) found that financial incentives did not promote significant weight loss or help to maintain weight loss, going against the idea of such incentives being a useful motivational tool. However, they did find that creating group contracts for weight loss does have some success, suggesting that social support has a motivational role to play.
- Miller-Kovach et al. (2001) reported that the social support methods that Weight Watchers offered were significantly superior to individual dieting regimes over a

period of 2 years, suggesting that creating social network support is a successful motivational device.

- Lowe et al. (2004) found that an average of 71.6% of Weight Watchers members maintained a body weight loss of at least 5%. This again indicates that the social support methods of the organisation motivate people to not only lose weight, but to maintain the loss.
- Bartlett (2003) found that dieting success occurs best with a target of reducing calorific intake of between 500 and a 1,000 calories a day, resulting in weight loss of about one to two pounds a week, supporting the idea that achievable goal-setting is a strong motivational force.
- Wing and Hill (2001) reported that common behaviours that led to successful weight loss and its maintenance included a low-fat diet, constant self-monitoring of food intake and weight and increased physical activity.

Explanations for failure

Diets often fail as they are unsustainable. Initial weight loss slows and weight is regained, the more restrictive the diet, the more likely it will fail. A prime factor is a lack of knowledge and skills necessary to diet sensibly. The unpleasant side effects of dieting, such as stress, can lead to loss of motivation and abandonment. People generally perceive dieting as a temporary restriction and then return to old eating habits and regain weight.

The hormone ghrelin plays a biological role. It stimulates appetite, making hungry people even hungrier during dieting, increasing the chances of abandonment. Cognitive factors play a role too, with a lessening of concentration having been associated with diets failing.

Research

- Jeffery (2000) found that obese people tend to start regaining weight after 6 months due to a failure to maintain behavioural changes, suggesting that factors like loss of motivation and social pressure have negative influences.
- Cummings et al. (2002) found that low-calorie diets stimulate appetite by increasing ghrelin production by 24%, reducing the chances of losing weight. The success of stomach-reduction surgery may be due to reduced stomachs producing less ghrelin.
- Williams et al. (2002) found that people who lack concentration are often unsuccessful with diets as they lose focus on targets and strategies, indicating that cognitive factors play a role in failure.
- However, D'Anci et al. (2008) found that it is low-carbohydrate diets that have a cognitive effect, reducing glycogen levels, causing a lack of concentration. This suggests it is certain types of diet that influence cognitive factors.

Evaluation

- Due to ethical concerns the types of research that can be conducted are restricted. For example setting up experimental designs could be problematic and thus self-reports are often used.

- Individual differences contribute to success rates. 'Low-restrainers' find dieting easy, while 'high-restrainers' find it difficult. Mensink et al. (2008) think high-restrainers are hyper-sensitive to food cues, thus likely to abandon diets. Stirling et al. (2004) found high-restrainers could not resist forbidden chocolate. However, it is not known whether being a high- or low-restrainer is innate or learned.
- Research findings will hopefully lead to the identification of strategies for successful dieting that can address the growing problem of obesity.
- Nolen-Hoeksema (2002) found that females on low-fat diets develop negative moods, which they address by over-eating, with 80% of these going on to develop clinical depression within 5 years. This suggests that dieting, rather than incurring positive results, can lead to a serious risk of developing mental disorders.

Biological explanations of eating behaviour

Specification content

- *Role of neural mechanisms involved in controlling eating and satiation*
- *Evolutionary explanations of food preference*

The focus of the specification is purely on how eating behaviour can be explained by internal biological mechanisms and processes and how our food preferences may have occurred via the process of evolution, thus providing an adaptive advantage. Neural mechanisms are specifically identified and therefore must be covered as they may feature specifically in an examination question. A thorough knowledge of evolutionary theory and how it can be applied to food preferences is also a requirement. Students should be adequately prepared to provide both descriptive and evaluative material on both these subject areas.

Role of neural mechanisms involved in controlling eating and satiation

Various neural mechanisms have been linked to the control of eating, with the hypothalamus being seen as the hunger centre of the brain. The ventromedial hypothalamus and the lateral hypothalamus have been identified as playing a key role and feature in both **Dual Control Theory** and **Set Point Theory**. Other areas of the limbic system may also have a part to play, indicating the complexity of biological factors in hunger and satiation. More contemporary research has indicated the contributory role that hormonal factors play.

Role of the hypothalamus

The hypothalamus has a critical role in the regulation of eating, acting like a thermostat to initiate or stop eating behaviour. The hypothalamus is a part of the limbic system. It links the nervous system to the endocrine system.

Dual Control Theory (DCT): this theory has a **homeostatic** view of hunger and satiety. When glucose levels fall the **lateral hypothalamus** (LH) is activated causing a sense of hunger that motivates a person to eat, which releases glucose. This activates the **ventromedial hypothalamus** (VMH), leading to a feeling of satiety and eating stops.

Research
- Hetherington and Ranson (1940) found that lesions to the VMH lead to hyperphagia (overeating) and weight gain. Anad and Brobeck (1951) found that lesions to the LH lead to aphagia (undereating) and weight loss, suggesting support for DCT.
- Stellar (1954) found the VMH, when stimulated, decreases eating but when lesioned, increases eating; while the LH, when stimulated and lesioned, produces the opposite effects. This indicates that, as predicted by DCT, these two brain areas are the feeding and satiety centres. However, the effects of lesioning may have been due to peripheral damage rather than damage to one specific area of the hypothalamus.
- Shaungshoti and Samranvej (1975) found a tumour had destroyed the VMH in a female exhibiting hyperphagia, supporting the findings of animal studies.
- Teitalbaum (1957) got rats to push a bar an increasing number of times to get food. Lesioned VMH rats initially work hard in line with DCT, but become less willing to work hard as more presses are required. It was also found that VMH lesioned rats are fussy eaters and eat less than normal rats if food tastes stale or bitter. These findings do not fit the predictions of DCT.

<blockquote>

Evaluation

- Lesioned VMH rats initially overeat and gain weight. However, these effects are temporary and body weight stabilises. DCT theory cannot explain these results as VMH rats are achieving satiety, even though their satiety centre is supposedly absent.
- Lesioned LH rats initially will not eat or drink and lose weight. However, these effects are also temporary and the ability to eat is regained, even though they have supposedly lost their hunger centre. Again DCT theory cannot explain these findings.

</blockquote>

Set Point Theory (SPT)

This was a solution to explaining the long-term effects of lesions to the VMH and LH. The theory perceives the role of the VMH and LH as controlling body weight by a set-point mechanism. SPT shows how lesioning the LH lowers the set-point for body weight, with body weight being maintained but at a lower level than before. While lesioning the VMH heightens the set-point, with body-weight being maintained but at a higher level than before.

Research
- Powley and Keesey (1970) found that rats that lose weight by being starved and then have lesions made to their LH do not lose further weight, supporting SPT as

it seems to indicate that the rats had slimmed down to a new set-point before the lesions were created.

- Proc and Frohman (1970) found that rats made obese through VMH lesioning and then force-fed to further increase body-weight lost weight when allowed to feed normally, supporting SPT, as the rats returned to their new increased set-point.

Evaluation

- Research has indicated that the neural mechanisms involved are complex. Ungerstedt (1971) found that lesions to the nigrostriatal tract (NGT), an area outside the LH, also produce aphagia.
- Perceiving the VMH as a satiety centre and the LH as a hunger centre is simplistic. Lesions to the LH also produce disruptions to aggression levels and sexual behaviour.

Hormonal factors

Various hormonal factors have been indicated as having important roles in the control of eating. **Glucostatic theory** sees brain mechanisms as monitoring blood-glucose levels, with glucoreceptors being located in the VMH. One source of glucose comes from the intestine producing **cholectystokinin (CCK)**, which activates the liver to release glucose and signals the brain. **Lipostatic theory** perceives reduced fat levels as causing hunger. The fat derived hormone **leptin** lowers activity in brain areas associated with hunger, while heightening them in areas associated with satiety.

Research

- Schneider and Tarshis (1995) found that lesioning the LH leads to body weight falling, as stored body fat is released to compensate for the fall in insulin production. As the blood stream is now energy rich, brain mechanisms believe eating is not required. This suggests that that the LH has a role in the control of insulin.
- Pinel (2000) showed that lesioned VMH rats have increased insulin levels, causing food to be converted to fat. The rats eat more to address the shortage of glucose in their blood stream, causing weight increase, suggesting that the VMH also plays a role in insulin control.

Evaluation

- Research has indicated that hormonal factors play key roles and has led to a better understanding of how eating is controlled.
- Quaade (1971) found that stimulating the VMH of obese people made them feel hungry. These results are similar to those of rats, suggesting that we can generalise findings onto humans.
- Wang (2006) found that the vagus nerve regulates hippocampus activity, which has an important role to play in modulating eating, indicating that other parts of the limbic system are also associated with hunger and satiety. Interestingly the same

areas are related to addiction cravings, suggesting similar neural circuits underlie desires for food and drugs in both addicts and the obese.

- Cognitive factors also have a role to play in determining satiety. We are aware we have eaten and therefore logically assume we are full.
- Confirmation of the prime function that the lipostatic theory plays, with a central role for the hormone leptin, was a major breakthrough and is a continuing area of research activity.
- The notion of a set point for body mass that is biologically determined has gained experimental support and has been used to create practical applications in the form of therapies to treat the obese.
- Research has tended to consist of artificial laboratory experiments, where animals are not allowed to eat freely, suggesting that results may not be ecologically valid.
- Due to practical and ethical constraints human studies are rare. However, findings from post-mortem studies have tended to lend support to animal studies.
- Many animal studies can be criticised on ethical grounds, for instance the distress that they cause. Such research would often now be difficult to justify on cost-benefit grounds, although it could be argued that research may lead to effective treatment of eating disorders.

Evolutionary explanations of food preference

Evolutionary theory sees food preferences as having evolved through natural selection due to environmental demands, as they have an adaptive advantage and therefore incur a survival value. Most human evolution occurred during the Pleistocene era, a time period known as the **Environment of Evolutionary Adaptiveness (EEA)**.

This was a time of nomadic hunter-gatherers, with food only periodically available, therefore humans evolved to favour energy rich foods and store excess as fat to help in times of scarcity. We still exhibit these behaviours and tendencies, even though food is perpetually available. Our food preferences therefore reflect our need for energy and stored nutrition and our need to avoid toxins.

Sweet tastes
These are generally indicative of high-energy and non-toxic content and would therefore be acted upon by natural selection to become a universal food preference.

Research
- Steiner (1979) used choice preferences and facial expressions to conclude that neonates prefer sweet tastes. However, interpreting neonates' behaviour is difficult and prone to bias. Beauchamp (1982) found that dietary experience modifies preferences for sweetness by as early as 6 months of age.
- De Araujo et al. (2008) found that mice that could not taste sweetness preferred a sugar solution rather than a non-calorific sweetener, suggesting the preference is based not on sweetness, but calorific content.

Evaluation

- A fondness for sweetness is common in the animal kingdom, lending support to it being an evolutionary preference.
- Stefansson (1960) reported that Copper Eskimos were disgusted at their first taste of sugar. This goes against the notion of sweetness being a universal preference.
- Zhao et al. (2008) found a genetic basis to sweetness preference and believe that variations in the preference can be explained by the variability of the genes in individuals rather than cultural differences.

Bitter and sour tastes

These tastes are indicative of toxins. Plants produce toxins to discourage being eaten and therefore it is evolutionary beneficial to develop an ability to detect and avoid bitter tastes.

Research

- Mennella (2008) found that children were more sensitive to bitter tastes than adults, suggesting that the preference is innate, with learned preferences overtaking inborn ones over time. It also explains why many children do not like bitter tasting vegetables and will not swallow bitter medicines.
- Simmen and Hladik (1998) found 27 receptors for bitter tastes but only two for sweet tastes, suggesting a different evolutionary importance between the need for energy and the need to avoid toxins.

Evaluation

- A practical application of the research is that children's medicines could have sweet tastes added to make them palatable.
- Environmental changes may be causing natural selection to reduce our ability to detect bitter tastes. Go et al. (2005) examined bitter-taste receptor genes in primates and found more pseudogenes (dead genes) in humans indicating human bitter tasting capabilities have deteriorated.
- Liem and Mennella (2003) found that 35% of children (but few adults) have a preference for sour taste, suggesting that these children are less food neophobic and will sample a greater variety of foods, incurring a selective advantage.

Salty tastes

Without sodium chloride we would dehydrate and die. A high sodium concentration is required in the bloodstream to maintain nerve and muscle activity.

Research

- Dudley et al. (2008) found that ants in inland, salt-poor environments prefer salty solutions to sugary ones, seemingly an adaptive response to maintain their evolutionary fitness.
- Beauchamp (1983) found that people with sodium deficiency have an innate response to ingest salt and find it more palatable and less aversive at high

concentrations than related family members. This indicates an evolutionary determined mechanism that helps maintenance of sodium levels, which has a high adaptive value.

Evaluation
- There are individual differences in salt preferences, which is puzzling as evolution would predict a standard universal preference.
- There may be a genetic basis to salt taste preferences. Zinner (2002) found that 23% of neonates had a preference for salty tastes, had a higher blood pressure and at least one grandparent with hypertension (indicative of high salt consumption). This could explain individual differences in salt preferences.
- Care must be taken when researching with neonates not to cause harm. For example in experimental conditions babies are not directly fed salt, instead they are exposed to small stimuli upon the tongue.

Meat
Meat is high in protein and energy-rich fat. Group hunting skills made it more available and cooking more palatable. Meat is also associated with a growth in human intelligence. Meat eating was risky and hunting was dangerous. Meat can be toxic and incur transmittable diseases.

Research
- Foley and Lee (1991) compared brain size with primate feeding strategies and concluded that meat eating led directly to the process of encephalisation, suggesting that evolution favoured meat eating in humans.
- Finch and Standford (2004) believe humans adapted to eat diverse foods, including meat, as it allowed them to exploit new environments, suggesting an adaptive advantage to meat eating.

Evaluation
- Kendrick (1980) found that longevity is associated with vegetarianism, suggesting that there is a cost to meat eating.
- Dunn (1990) points out that our dental structures and digestive systems are more similar to herbivores than carnivores and that true carnivores eat meat raw, guts and all, suggesting we do not have an innate preference for meat.
- The American Academy of Paediatrics (1998) point out that neonates can only ingest milk; meat is a late introduction to our diet and neophobics tend to dislike meat. This does not suggest an evolutionary determined preference for meat eating.

Variety
An innate preference for a variety of foods would be beneficial as it would increase food supplies, allow variation in times of scarcity and allow ingestion of a wide range of vitamins and minerals.

Research

- Davis (1928) found that children prefer a wide range of food, suggesting an evolutionary determined preference. However, Sclafani and Springer (1976) offered a wider range of foods to rats but they only ate junk foods and became obese. It may not be possible to generalise to humans.

Evaluation

- Having a preference for variety would mean liking new foods that may be poisonous.
- Food neophobia indicates variety has not been determined by evolution.
- There may be an innate ability to develop learned food aversions. Garcia et al. (1966) found that rats made sick by an injection reject whatever food they ate just before they were sick. This ability would have a selective advantage.
- Cuisine may affect adaptive fitness as a form of bio-cultural evolution. Katz (1982) reports that Native Americans who use an alkali solution when preparing corn consumed more corn in their diet, allowing more nutrition to be extracted.
- The evolutionary concept of adaptiveness can be applied to many behaviours, but as it is an explanation of how things have come to be, it is difficult to prove or disprove by usual research methods.

Eating disorders

Specification content

- *Psychological explanations of one eating disorder, for example anorexia nervosa, bulimia nervosa, obesity*
- *Biological explanations, including neural and evolutionary explanations, for one eating disorder, for example anorexia nervosa, bulimia nervosa, obesity*

The emphasis in this section is solely on eating disorders. There is a requirement to have a knowledge of psychological explanations, although which ones are studied and used to answer examination questions is totally a free choice, no specific one is named. There is also a requirement to have a knowledge of biological explanations, including neural and evolutionary explanations as they are specifically named.

It is important to note you must have knowledge of psychological and biological explanations relating to just one eating disorder; again there is a totally free choice. You will not be set a question that requires you to address a particular eating disorder. Due to constraints of space, this guide will concentrate on just one eating disorder: obesity. Suffice to say that any other eating disorder would be equally acceptable.

Obesity

When fat accumulates to an extent that body mass index (BMI) is $30kg/m^2$, then a person is defined as clinically obese. In Britain (2008) 24% of people are obese. Levels are increasing worldwide and in the USA it is the second biggest cause of preventable death, being linked to cardiovascular diseases, diabetes etc. with 9% of health costs being attributed to the condition. Various factors may contribute to obesity and only by gaining insight into the condition can it be successfully addressed.

Psychological explanations

Psychodynamic

Obesity is seen as due to unresolved conflicts, such as emotional deprivation during the oral stage. The libido then becomes locked onto oral gratification. Obesity may also be linked to other factors that are explicable by psychodynamic means, for instance, depression.

Research

- Felliti (2001) reported on five cases of sleep-eating obesity (eating food while asleep). All had suffered abuse in childhood and their behaviour can be interpreted as an unconscious anxiety reducer, backing up the theory.

Evaluation

- Most obese people have not suffered abuse or indulge in sleep eating, suggesting the psychodynamic explanation can only account for a few cases at best.
- Obesity has grown to epidemic proportions, but there is no evidence of a parallel rise in unresolved childhood conflicts, casting doubt on the explanation.
- Cases of depression etc. linked to obesity may actually be an effect of obesity rather than a cause.

Behavioural explanations

Obesity is seen as a maladaptive, learned behaviour occurring through overeating in three possible ways:

Classical conditioning: obesity occurs because food is naturally associated with pleasure and food cues come to be associated with a pleasurable response.

Operant conditioning: obesity is seen as occurring due to food being used as a reinforcer (reward) for desirable behaviour.

Social learning theory: obesity is seen as being caused by the observation and imitation of obese role models.

Research

- Foster (2006) reports that treatments based on classical conditioning are successful as they help patients identify cues triggering inappropriate eating and then learn new responses to them. Therefore causes may be due to classical conditioning.
- Jackson (2008) reports that reinforcing children for eating creates a compulsion leading to obesity, which suggests operant conditioning in childhood is to blame.
- Hardeman et al. (2000) reports that treating obesity by role models encouraging healthy lifestyles led to significant weight loss, lending support to behavioural explanations.

Evaluation

- Treatments based on classical conditioning create specific goals and identify clearly what is required. Wing et al. (2002) found such treatments incur average weight loss of 15.6 kg in 18 months, suggesting such treatments do work.
- Operant conditioning techniques have also been used to treat obesity by reinforcing more healthy practices. Devlin et al. (1995) found that weight loss was not maintained, suggesting that operant conditioning does not explain the causes of obesity.
- Weight loss, after treatments based on social learning theory, tends to be short term, indicating that other psychological and biological explanations should be considered.

Cognitive explanations

Cognitive theory sees obesity occurring as a result of maladaptive thought processes, with information processing having an elevated focus for food related stimuli.

Research

- Braet and Crombez (2001) found that obese children were hypersensitive to food related words, suggesting an information processing bias for food stimuli, leading to obesity.
- Cserjesi et al. (2007) examined cognitive profiles of obese boys and found them deficient in attention capabilities, suggesting that childhood obesity involves cognitive deficits.

Evaluation

- Attention deficits may be an effect of being obese. Elias (2003) found that early-onset, long-term obesity leads to a decline in cognitive functioning. This weakens the cognitive explanation as a cause of obesity.
- The success of therapies based on the cognitive approach suggests that cognitive factors may be involved in developing obesity. O'Rourke et al. (2008) found that cognitive-behavioural therapy significantly improved weight loss.

Biological explanations

Genetic

Some individuals may be more genetically predisposed to become obese and having multiple genes that are linked to obesity will increase the chances of the condition developing.

Research

- Frayling et al. (2007) found that people with two copies of the fat mass and obesity gene (FTO) had a 70% chance of becoming obese, while those with one copy had just a 30% chance, supporting the idea of having multiple genes increasing the chances of being obese.
- Wardle et al. (2008) assessed twins on BMI and body fat deposits and found a heritability figure of 77%, suggesting that genetic factors have a major influence on obesity.

- Sorensen and Stunkard (1994) compared the degree of obesity of adopted participants with that of their adoptive and biological parents and found an individual's weight was more correlated with biological relatives, lending support to the genetic explanation.
- Willer et al. (2008) have located new genes associated with obesity. These variant genes increase the chances of being obese by up to 25%, suggesting genes do play a role in creating a predisposition to obesity.

Evaluation

- Musani et al. (2008) has suggested that obese people may be more fertile, reproduce more and ultimately increase genes favouring obesity in the population.
- Most cases of obesity cannot be explained by genetics alone. Genes do not determine obesity, they need an environment in which to express themselves.
- Genes cannot explain the upsurge in obesity. Genes have not changed, but environmental factors, like the availability of food have, suggesting environment plays the larger role.
- The discovery of genes related to obesity may lead to the construction of effective gene therapies for the treatment of the condition.

Neural

The hypothalamus, which has been identified with playing a key role in the regulation of eating, has been associated with the development of obesity. Specific neural circuits have been investigated, as well as associated hormones and neurotransmitters.

Research

- Friedman (2005) reports that two hypothalamic neurons, NPY and POMC, are the key regulators of appetite and therefore play a key role in establishing weight. These neurons are controlled mainly by leptin. This hormone increases as a person gains weight, washing over the POMC neuron to decrease appetite. As weight is lost, leptin levels decrease and the NPY neuron dominates, increasing appetite. Obese people do produce leptin, but its ability to suppress the neuron POMC is blocked and so their appetite stays high and they gain weight up to a point that is thought to be genetically determined.
- Stice et al. (2008) reports that obese people have fewer dopamine receptors in the brain. They tend to overeat to compensate for having a poorly functioning dorsal striatum, which leads to lessened dopamine signalling in the brain. This implies that the neurotransmitter dopamine may be linked to obesity.
- Reeves and Plum (1969) conducted a post-mortem on an obese female and found her VMH had been destroyed, suggesting that the hypothalamus is associated with the development of obesity.

Evaluation

- The evidence linking dopamine to obesity tends to be correlational and so it is not clear if dopamine is a cause or an effect of being obese.

- It was hoped that leptin injections might prove an effective treatment for obesity, but they only work for a few people, casting doubt on the importance of leptin's role.
- A lot of research into leptin was carried out on mice and so the results may not be generalisable to humans.

Evolutionary

Our eating habits are more suited to the EEA where food was not universally available. We evolved to find high calorific foods desirable and store excess energy as fat for times of scarcity. We may have also evolved to minimise physical activity in order to preserve fat stores. Therefore we are not suited to a sedentary world of ever-available fatty foods. We may be vulnerable to over-eating foods that were not part of our evolutionary past, because they do not trigger neural mechanisms that control appetite.

The **thrifty gene model** believes that there was a selective advantage for people with insulin resistance as they would have been able to metabolise food more efficiently. This was advantageous in times of food scarcity, but now food is ever available it leads to obesity.

Research

- Bray et al. (2004) found that high fructose corn syrup (HFCS) may be a major cause of obesity. It is used to sweeten drinks in the USA and consumption has increased by 1000% between 1970 and 1990. This was not a foodstuff consumed in our evolutionary past and it is seen as not stimulating leptin and insulin production, which normally act to regulate eating and therefore leads to weight gain.
- DiMeglio and Mates (2000) found that participants put on more weight when given liquid calories rather than an equal amount of solid calories. This backs up the idea that liquid calories have caused the huge increase in obesity because we are not shaped by evolution to cope with them.
- Rowe et al. (2007) studied the genetics of modern day Pima Indians who have high levels of obesity and concluded that they have a thrifty metabolism that allows them to metabolise food more efficiently. This was once an advantage in times of food scarcity, but now leads to obesity, lending support to the thrifty gene hypothesis.
- Friedman et al. (1994) studied the islanders of Kosrae where obesity levels have rocketed. It was concluded that the thrifty gene was well represented among the population and due to the constant availability of abundant food in modern times, obesity has become a major problem. The small percentage that remain lean are seen as not having the gene. It is believed that each person has a genetically determined 'set-point' and we are motivated to keep eating until we reach it. Due to high levels of the thrifty gene the islanders have higher than average set-points.

Evaluation

- The evolutionary view offers a plausible explanation for modern levels of obesity and why people find losing weight difficult. Our bodies are designed to consume as much as possible and lay down fat stores.

- The thrifty gene hypothesis can explain why people who do not have the gene are able to eat lots and not put on weight.
- Monsivais et al. (2007) has cast doubts on the idea of foodstuffs not part of our evolutionary past being a cause of obesity, because obesity levels have also risen in countries where HFCS is not commonly used.
- The evolutionary approach, rather than being genetically determinist and seeing no role for other factors, is an interactionist viewpoint, seeing eating behaviour as being caused by a mixture of genetic and environmental factors. Therefore the approach is not being reductionist as it acknowledges the influence of more than a single factor.
- By understanding the adaptive significance of obesity, it may be possible to develop practical applications that successfully treat the condition.

Hormonal

An increasing feature of research is what role various hormones play in the development of obesity. **Insulin** has attracted interest for its role in directing the storage and utilisation of energy. **Cortisol** has also attracted attention due to its powerful metabolic effects. **Ghrelin** has been investigated as its secretion stimulates eating.

Research

- Kahn and Flier (2000) have found that insulin resistance coupled with a large consumption of high-glycemic foods, often found in junk foods, can lead to obesity. Therefore insulin resistance does not seem to be a sole cause.
- Epel et al. (2001) found that women with high levels of cortisol overeat sweet foods, suggesting a role for cortisol in increasing levels of body fat leading to obesity.
- Shintani et al. (2001) found that the action of ghrelin does not have a direct influence, but is caused instead by the production of leptin, which in turn is controlled through increased action of the NPY. This suggests neural factors may be more important.

Evaluation

- It is not clear as yet whether abnormal levels of cortisol are a cause or an effect of obesity.
- Evidence seems to suggest that hormonal factors play a contributory role in developing obesity rather than being direct causes.

Perception

Theories of perceptual organisation

Specification content

- *Gregory's top down/indirect theory of perception*
- *Gibson's bottom up/direct theory of perception*

The focus of the specification is precise and straightforward: to have a knowledge and understanding of these two major theories of perceptual organisation. Questions set on this part of the specification will concentrate specifically on these two theories and you must be able to evaluate them and describe them. Questions may be set on one theory alone, but it would be perfectly legitimate for a question to be set that requires you to compare the theories.

Sensation and perception are two separate, but linked processes. Perception cannot happen without sensations, but sensations have no meaning on their own. Theories of perceptual organisation seek to explain the relationship between these two processes. Either we perceive the world directly from sensory information (Gibson) or we use sensory information to infer perception based on previous experience (Gregory).

Gregory's top down/indirect theory

Perception is seen as actively searching for the best interpretation of sensory data based on previous experience and therefore involves going beyond the immediate data. We learn to perceive by interacting with our world. Perception is an unconscious process and occurs indirectly, as it involves higher level (top-down) processing.

Gregory believes a lot of sensory data is impoverished, incomplete or ambiguous and therefore we need to go beyond it, making inferences in order to perceive, although sometimes this can lead to errors, for instance visual illusions.

The idea of **perceptual set** is crucial to Gregory's theory. It is a readiness to perceive certain features of sensory data based on previous experience, motivational and emotional factors and cultural influences.

Expectation

This is a feature of Gregory's theory where we perceive what we expect to see based on previous experience.

Research

- Aarts and Dijksterhuis (2002) influenced estimates of a man's walking speed by creating an expectation of what it should be, by first asking participants to think about fast or slow animals. This shows how experience can bias perception, demonstrating that it is both an indirect and active process, providing support for the idea of perceptual set.
- Leeper (1935) showed participants an ambiguous picture, which could either be seen as a young or an old woman. It was found that participants initially given a description or picture of a young woman saw a young woman and those described or shown an old woman saw an old woman. This indicates that expectation based on previous experience can determine perception in an indirect fashion.

Motivational and emotional factors

These can affect perception by creating a bias to perceive, or not, certain features of the incoming sensory data. **Perceptual defence** is an important concept here, where emotionally threatening stimuli take longer to perceive.

Research

- McGinnies (1949) found that emotionally threatening words took longer to recognise than neutral ones, lending support to the idea of perceptual defence and emotional factors influencing perception. However, the results may have been due to the embarrassment of speaking the words aloud. Bitterman and Kniffin (1953) found no differences in recognition time if the words were written down.
- Lazarus and McCleary (1951) found that nonsense syllables presented so fast they could not be consciously perceived raised anxiety levels if they had previously been paired with electric shocks. This supports the idea of emotional factors unconsciously influencing perception.
- Solley and Haigh (1948) found that children drew a bigger Santa and sack of toys as Christmas approached, but after it had passed Santa and his sack shrunk. This indicates that motivational factors influence perception.
- Balcettis and Dunning (2006) flashed, briefly, an ambiguous figure that could either be seen as the letter 'B' or the number '13'. Participants, who were told that a letter would get them a nice drink, perceived the letter, while those told a number would earn them the drink, perceived the number. This supports the idea that perceptual set influences perception in an indirect fashion and we see what we wish to see.

Cultural influences

These influence perceptual set by predisposing people to perceive features of an environment in a certain way. Therefore people from different cultural backgrounds can sometimes perceive identical sensory information differently. Gregory explained how the Müller-Lyer illusion (where, out of two equal lines, A appears longer than B; (see Figure 1) is seen by people of some cultures, but not others. People of a Western culture live in a carpentered world of manufactured straight lines, angles etc. while some cultures only have buildings made from natural materials. Therefore a person from a Western culture experiences the illusion, because they unconsciously read the third dimension of depth into it from experience.

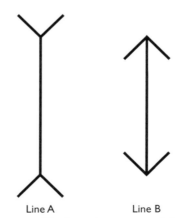

Line A   Line B

Figure 1 The Müller-Lyer illusion. Does one of the lines seem longer?

Research

- Pettigrew et al. (1978) presented a picture of one South African ethnic group to one eye of a participant and another ethnic group to the other eye. White South Africans were not able to distinguish between black and mixed-race people, suggesting that the cultural influence of their racial prejudice affected their perception.
- Segall (1963) found that Africans, who lived in open country where occasional vertical objects were important features, were susceptible to the horizontal-vertical illusion, while those living in dense jungle were unlikely to see the illusion. This implies that our physical environment shapes cultural influences, which affects our perception.

Evaluation

- The theory has helped us to understand perception better and has stimulated interest and research in the subject area.
- There is a wealth of research evidence, both experimental and naturalistic supporting Gregory's theory.
- There is a logical sense to the theory that we would make inferences based on previous experience when viewing conditions are incomplete or ambiguous.
- A methodological criticism is that laboratory experiments are biased to favour Gregory's theory. Fragmented and briefly presented stimuli are often used and so it would be difficult to perceive directly from the sensory data.
- Generally peoples' perceptions, even those from different cultures, tend to be similar. If it were true that we build our individual perceptions from our individual experiences, this would not be so. This weakens support for Gregory's theory.
- Gregory possibly underestimates how rich and informative sensory data is and that therefore it may be possible to perceive directly from it. This misbelief could have arisen because laboratory experiments present incomplete or isolated stimuli, while in the real world sensory data is more informative and complete.
- According to Gregory's theory once we understand why we experience an illusion our perception would be modified and we would not experience it anymore. However, we still do, casting doubt onto Gregory's explanation.
- The theory suggests we need to search through memory to find the best interpretation of incoming sensory data. However, this would be a time-consuming and inefficient method of perceiving and again casts doubts on how Gregory sees perception as occurring.
- Eysenck and Keane (1990) believe Gregory's theory is better at explaining the perception of illusions than real objects, because illusions are unreal and simplified and so easy to make mistakes over, while real objects provide enough complex data for them to be perceived directly.

Gibson's bottom up/direct theory of perception

Gibson believes that the **optic array** (the pattern of light hitting our eyes) is a rich enough source of sensory data for us to perceive directly. Our own movements and those of surrounding objects within an environment facilitate this process. This involves innate mechanisms forged by evolution and therefore we do not need to learn from experience.

Gibson believes that perception occurs due to direct perception of **invariants**, features of the optical array that remain constant and that contain enough sensory information to allow direct perception — for instance, depth, distance and spatial arrangements. No inferences from previous experience are necessary or any higher information processing. It is a bottom-up process as we construct perception directly from sensory information. In contrast to Gregory, Gibson sees the perceiver not as the brain, but as the person within their environment. The function of perception therefore is to enable an animal to function in its environment in safety.

The optical array

The optical array is composed of structured (patterned) light that hits our eyes. It is an ever-changing source of sensory information due to the movements of ourselves and objects within our physical environment. The optical array contains **invariant** elements, which are constant sources of information. There are several types of invariants, all of which contribute to allow us to perceive directly from the sensory information.

Optic flow patterns

From his work with pilots Gibson described optic flow patterns as unambiguous sources of information concerning height, distance and speed that directly inform perception. As we move about in our environment, distant objects appear to move slowly, while closer objects seem to move more quickly. This depth cue is known as **motion parallax**.

Research

- Bardy et al. (1996) asked participants to walk on a treadmill that had a screen in front onto which optic flow patterns were beamed. It was found that motion parallax was used to maintain balance by using optic flow patterns to make compensatory movements, supporting Gibson's idea that optic flow patterns are rich enough sources of information to allow direct perception.
- Johansson (1973) found that a black clad actor wearing lights on his knees, ankles etc, walking in a darkened room, was perceivable as a moving person, but a stationary person was not perceivable if he was stood still. This shows how important movement is in determining optic flow patterns.
- Maher and West (1993) filmed the movements of black-clad animals with lights on their joints and found that the species of animal was recognisable to an observer. This demonstrates how strong a source of information movement is in determining optic flow patterns and shows that there is enough sensory information for perception to occur directly.

Texture gradient

This is a surface pattern that provides sensory information concerning the depth, shape etc. of an object. Physical objects possess surfaces with different textures that allow the direct perception of distance, depth and spatial awareness. Due to movements the 'flow' of texture gradients provides a rich source of sensory information. Motion parallax and **linear perspective**, a depth cue provided by lines seeming to converge as they get further away, allow the third dimension of depth to be directly available to the senses.

Research

- Gibson and Bridgeman (1987) showed participants photographs of surface textures. Participants were able to correctly identify objects, state their colour, identify the light conditions and say whether they were lying flat etc. suggesting that there is sufficient sensory information in surface textures to permit direct perception. This therefore supports Gibson's theory.
- Frichtel et al. (2006) presented participants with a film of a car driving through scenery. Evidence was found that infants as young as 4 months of age could perceive by using texture gradient, implying that the ability may be innate, therefore lending support to Gibson's theory that perception is reliant on innate mechanisms.

Horizon ratios

Horizon ratios concern the position of an object in relation to the horizon. Objects of different sizes at equal distances from an observer have different horizon ratios. Therefore horizon ratios provide another source of invariant sensory information allowing direct perception.

Research

- Creem-Regehr et al. (2003) found that restricting participants' viewing conditions did not significantly affect their ability to judge distances using horizon-ratio information, suggesting that this form of invariant sensory information is a powerful tool in establishing direct perception.

Affordances

Affordances involve attaching meaning to sensory information. It is the quality of an object that permits actions to be carried out upon it (action possibilities), for example a brush 'affords' sweeping the floor. Affordances were seen by Gibson as being directly perceivable and thus rejects Gregory's belief that the meaning of objects is stored in long-term memory from experience.

Research

- Warren (1984) studied whether participants could judge if staircases portrayed with differently proportioned steps could 'afford' to be climbed. Whether they could was dependent on the length of a participant's leg. It was found that participants were sensitive to the affordance of 'climbability' and according to Gibson this would be achieved by the invariant properties of the light reflected from the staircases. This provides some support for the concept of affordances not being reliant on experience.
- Bruce and Green (1990) found that the idea of affordances could be used to explain the visually controlled behaviour of animals like insects, lending some

support to Gibson's theory. However, unlike humans such animals are not thought to require an internal, conceptual representation of their environment.

Evaluation

- A practical application of Gibson's theory is putting parallel lines increasingly closer together as a road junction nears, giving a false impression of speed to slow drivers down.
- Gibson's theory has led to greater understanding, interest and research into perception. For instance Gaver (1996) has applied the idea of affordances into designing computer displays.
- There may be a biological basis to Gibson's theory. Logothetis and Pauls (1995) identified neurons in the brains of monkeys that seemed to perceive specific objects regardless of their orientation, implying a biological mechanism that allows direct perception.
- Gibson's theory can explain how we can perceive so quickly, which Gregory's theory cannot do.
- Gibson cannot really explain why we perceive illusions; he dismissed them as artificial laboratory constructions viewed under restrictive conditions. But some illusions occur naturally under normal viewing conditions.
- The idea that the optical array provides direct information about what objects allow us to do (affordances) seems unlikely. Our knowledge about objects is affected by cultural influences, experience and emotions.
- Perhaps a combination of Gregory's top-down and Gibson's bottom–up ideas would form the best explanation of perception. Gibson's theory works best for ideal viewing conditions, while Gregory's works best for less then ideal conditions. This approach was utilised in Neisser's (1976) 'Perceptual Cycle' theory.

Development of perception

Specification content

- *Development of perceptual abilities, for example depth/distance, visual constancies. Infant and cross-cultural studies of the development of perceptual abilities*
- *Nature–nurture debate in relation to explanations of perceptual development*

Knowledge of how perceptual abilities develop is required. The abilities listed in the specification are not definite requirements as they are just examples and therefore could not be explicitly referred to in an examination question. However, there is a wealth of research evidence on the examples named, so they would form a good focus of study. As infant and cross-cultural studies are specifically identified, there is a particular requirement to have a knowledge and understanding of what they are and what they tell us about perceptual development. You are required not only to have a knowledge of what the nature–nurture debate is, but to be able to specifically relate it to explanations of perceptual development.

Development of perceptual abilities

Perception is not a single entity, but is made up of several abilities, some of which are more learned in nature, while others are more innate. A baby is born with some basic perceptual abilities that have an immediate survival value and allow it to interact with its environment. In this way perceptual abilities can become shaped to suit an individual's needs and environment and therefore complex abilities tend to be affected more by learning. Research has concentrated on individual perceptual abilities with a regard to assessing what proportion are learned or innate. Various methodologies have been employed, each with its strengths and weaknesses.

Perceptual abilities

Depth/distance involves the ability to perceive the environment as three-dimensional and to judge distances of objects from each other and ourselves. There are two types of depth/distance cues: **monocular** (apparent to one eye) and **binocular** (apparent to both eyes) (see Table 7). The cues can also be divided into **primary** (not dependent on learning) and **secondary** (dependent on learning). Primary cues tend to get used by infants as they are innate and therefore appear first.

Table 7 Types of distance/depth cues

Primary cues	Description	Secondary cues	Description
Retinal disparity Binocular cue	Information from both eyes is combined to give impression of depth and distance	Interposition Binocular cue	When objects overlap, fully visible one is nearer
Convergence Binocular cue	Feedback from eye-muscles when focusing on objects informs about depth and distance	Texture gradient Binocular cue	Changes in texture gradients inform about depth and distance
Accommodation Monocular cue	Feedback from the curvature of the lens informs about depth and distance	Retinal size Binocular cue	The size of retinal images informs about depth and distance
		Motion parallax Binocular cue	Perceiving objects moving at different speeds informs about depth and distance
		Ariel perspective Monocular cue	Sharp images are seen as closer. Blurry ones as further away
		Elevation Monocular cue	Concerns an object's placement in relation to the horizon
		Linear perspective Monocular cue	Lines appear to converge into the distance and objects appear to shrink

Visual constancies concern how objects appear to remain constant and unchanging regardless of the viewing conditions (see Table 8). This has an adaptive survival value, as an ordered, predictable world is a safer place to interact with.

Table 8 Visual constancies

Type of visual constancy	Description
Size constancy	Familiar objects appear to have a constant size regardless of the retinal image
Shape constancy	Familiar objects retain a constant shape regardless of changes in the viewing angle
Brightness constancy	The perceived brightness of a familiar object remains constant despite the viewing conditions
Colour constancy	Familiar objects appear to retain their colour regardless of the lighting conditions

Neonate studies

Whatever perceptual abilities are present at birth are assumed to be innate, as learning experiences will not have occurred. Neonate studies present ethical and practical challenges and various methodologies have been developed, such as *preference studies* (which stimuli is preferred), **sucking, heart/breathing rate** (indicates interest), **reinforcement** (to show recognition), **brain scans** (to show neural activity).

Research

Depth/distance perception

- Gibson and Walk (1960) found that babies would not cross an apparent vertical drop. Neonate animals would not cross either, suggesting that depth perception is innate.
- Bower et al. (1970) found that neonates shielded their eyes at approaching objects. This suggests depth perception is innate. The findings were the same with only one eye, indicating that motion parallax is an important visual cue in determining depth.
- Slater et al. (1984) found that neonates prefer to look at a three-dimensional stimulus than a photograph of the same stimulus, even with just one eye. Motion parallax is again important and the research suggests depth perception is innate or develops soon after birth.
- Sen et al. (2001) using a visual illusion found that 7-month-old but not 5½-month-old infants, using monocular vision, would reach for the apparent end of a cylinder. This suggests that the ability to perceive static monocular depth cues occurs around 6 months of age.

Visual constancies

Shape

Imura et al. (2008) found that 7-month-old but not 6-month-old infants had a preference for an alternating 2D–3D display than a 2D–2D one, suggesting that sensitivity to shading and line junctions as a means of determining shape constancy appears between 6 and 7 months of age.

Size

Bower (1966) trained infants by reinforcement to respond to a certain cube at a certain distance. Various other cubes of differing sizes and at various distances were then presented. The infants mainly responded to the cube of the same size, regardless of its retinal image, suggesting that size constancy occurs early in life. Variations of his experiment led to Bower finding that motion parallax was the most important cue and that texture gradient was not used to determine size.

Sann and Steri (2007) investigated shape constancy through vision and touch. Neonates could recognise visually an object they had held, but could not recognise by touch alone an object previously seen. This indicates that the sensory modes used to perceive shape constancy differ in how much they are learned or innate.

Brightness

Chien (2003) tested 4-month-old infants on a novelty-preference task based on brightness and found that they could judge relative brightness of objects and their surroundings, indicating support for brightness constancy being innate.

Chien (2006) using smiley faces as stimuli found that infants displayed brightness constancy even when the level of lighting altered, again suggesting that this constancy is innate.

Colour

Dannemiller and Hanko (1987) found that 4-month-old infants could recognise familiar colours under some conditions, but not all, indicating that some colour constancy appears early in life, but needs time to develop fully.

Pereverzeva and Teller (2004) tested infants' preferences to stimuli of various colours embedded in a white or dark surround. The infants preferred stimuli where there was the greatest difference in colour between the stimulus and the surround, suggesting that they did have colour constancy.

Evaluation

- The visual system of a neonate is not well developed at birth, which makes finding what skills are innate problematic.
- Neonate studies can often be criticised as older infants are actually used and they may have learned perceptual abilities from experience.
- There are ethical considerations with neonate studies of informed consent and especially causing distress. For example Gibson and Walk got mothers to try and call babies across a visual cliff, which was distressing.
- Neonate studies often involve making inferences about their perceptual world. However, these may not be accurate and could be prone to researcher bias.
- Neonates lose concentration easily so research tends to be short term and so results may not be valid.

- Innate abilities may not be apparent at birth, but emerge later as a result of biological maturation without any learning required.

Cross-cultural studies

Cross-cultural studies involve testing people from different cultures on the same variables. If people from different cultures have similar perceptual abilities, then it is seen as evidence that those abilities are innate. Conversely if abilities are different, then it is assumed they have been learned.

One popular form of study is to compare people from widely differing cultural environments on their responses to visual illusion.

Research

- Turnbull (1961) befriended a pygmy who lived in dense forest with no experience of long-distance vision. When taken to savannah grasslands the pygmy thought distant buffalo were insects, suggesting the depth cues necessary for size constancy are learned.
- Hudson (1960) showed various cultural groups a 2D picture that contained depth cues. He found that children from all cultures had initial difficulty in perceiving depth in the picture. Those who subsequently had experience of such pictures learned to interpret the depth cues, suggesting that depth perception in pictures is a learned skill.
- Montello (2006) performed a meta-analysis of cross-cultural studies of depth/distance and found cultural differences to be fairly small, supporting the idea that these perceptual abilities are innate and have evolved as they have a survival value. The fact that some differences were found suggests that the ability has the capacity to be modified by experience.
- Segall et al. (1963) showed various illusions to different cultural groups. Europeans were found more likely to experience the Müller-Lyer illusion, while Zulus tended not to, suggesting that because Europeans have had experience of a carpentered world of straight lines and angles, they have learned to read the depth cues present in their environment, while the Zulus have not.
- Allport and Pettigrew (1957) found that people of a Western culture perceive an illusion caused by a rotating trapezoid, because they interpret it as a window. Rural Zulus, who have no experience of windows, do not perceive the illusion, supporting the idea that perceptual abilities are learned through environmental experiences.

Evaluation

- Research on illusions that suggests environment determines perception has been criticised. Pollack and Silva (1967) found Europeans are more susceptible to the Müller-Lyer illusion because their retinas allow them to detect contours better, suggesting a biological reason for cultural differences in perception of the illusion.
- The use of depth cues in pictures as a research tool has been criticised, as they do not relate to the actual world. Cox (1992) showed how Aboriginal art cannot be understood by other cultures unless the 'code' behind it is learned.
- Cross-cultural studies are susceptible to biased interpretation, especially in terms of the culture of the researcher.

- Cross-cultural research has focused mainly on visual illusions, which may not relate to more everyday perceptual abilities.
- It is often difficult with cross-cultural studies to obtain similar samples and replicate the methodology exactly. This can decrease the validity of findings.

Nature–nurture debate in relation to explanations of perceptual development

The nature–nurture debate concerns whether human qualities are innate (genetic) or learned (environmental) and development of abilities is seen as occurring either due to biological maturation (nature) or through experience (nurture). Some perceptual abilities seem more innate, while others seem more learned.

The more realistic view is that of **interactionism**, where perceptual skills are seen as being a combination of innate and learned factors. Basic skills tend to be innate and useful for immediate survival, while more complex skills are learned and modifiable to suit different and changing environments.

Generally Gibson's theory favours the nature side of the argument, as Gibson does not believe we need environmental experiences to perceive. Gregory's theory, which does see a role for environmental experiences, favours nurture.

Neonate and cross-cultural studies generally indicate that we have basic innate skills and that these are refined through experience (see neonate and cross-cultural studies earlier for details).

Animal studies

Animal studies often use sensory deprivation to determine what (if any) sensory experiences are necessary for perceptual development.

Research

- Hubel and Weisel (1962) tested pattern recognition in cats by surgically implanting electrodes in the visual cortex and found specialist neurons for specific perceptual tasks, suggesting that recognising patterns has a biological basis, therefore supporting the nurture viewpoint.
- Hubel and Weisel (1982) found that innate perceptual skills need environmental experience to develop fully. If a kitten's eye was sewn up early enough and long enough, the eye became blind, showing how nature and nurture interact to form perceptual abilities.
- Reisen (1965) fitted goggles to chimps that allowed light through, but not patterned light. Many perceptual abilities, such as tracking moving objects, did not develop fully, suggesting that the environmental experience of seeing patterned light is required to develop complex perceptual skills. This supports nature.

Evaluation

- There are problems generalising from animal studies to humans. Human perception may consist of more complex skills, which evidence suggests need more environ-

mental input to develop fully. Human perception may be more modifiable too; animals tend not to be able to adjust to new perceptual realities, while humans sometimes can.
- The physical and psychological harm caused by animal experiments raises ethical concerns. Use of a cost-benefit analysis can sometimes be used to justify their use, for instance if such research led to successful treatments for visual impairments.

Perceptual readjustment studies

These studies attempt to see if it is possible to adapt to a different perceptual world. If it is, then this is taken as evidence to support nurture.

Research
- Sperry (1943) found that salamanders could not adjust to a new perceptual world after having their eyes rotated to an upside-down position, favouring the nature side of the debate.
- Hess (1956) found similar results by fitting prisms to chicken's eyes that shifted images to one side. They were unable to adjust, which again supports nature.
- Snyder and Pronko (1952) put inversing-reversing goggles on participants and found they could adjust to an upside-down, back-to-front world, suggesting the ability was learned and thus supporting the nature viewpoint.

Evaluation
- Studies seem to show that humans can re-adjust. However, they may actually have learned to adapt their motor responses rather than adapt their perceptual abilities, casting doubt on the nature side of the debate.
- Research shows that humans can make perceptual re-adjustments. As an innate system would not permit this, it suggests that learning plays a major role in the development of perception, supporting nature.

Cataract studies

When people have cataracts removed from their eyes, whatever perceptual abilities they exhibit are assumed to be innate.

Research
- Gregory and Wallace (1963) reported on a case study of a man with cataracts from birth that were removed at age 52. He could visually recognise objects known from touch, but could not learn to recognise new objects by vision alone and he could not learn to judge distances. As he could not adjust, this is evidence for nature.
- Von Senden (1960) reviewed 65 cataract removal cases. Patients tended to be initially confused and although they learned to track moving objects and distinguish between objects and backgrounds, they generally did not adjust to their new perceptual world, again supporting the nature argument.

Evaluation
- Case studies of people with cataracts are rare and therefore may not be represen-tative. Most cataract patients have had visual experiences from before they

developed cataracts and therefore their perceptual abilities, evident when cataracts are removed, may not be innate.

- Physical damage to the visual system may have occurred during the time of blindness and this factor may be responsible for the lack of perceptual abilities, casting doubts on the validity of conclusions drawn from cataract removal studies.

The nature–nurture debate is difficult to resolve. Different research methods can often produce conflicting results, possibly because perception should not be researched as a whole ability, but as a series of inter-related individual abilities, with each one being studied separately. The different research methodologies each have their drawbacks too, for instance the problem of generalising from animal studies, or just what neonates can actually see. In conclusion, the best understanding of the debate comes from one that considers an input from both nature and nurture.

Face recognition and visual agnosias

Specification content

- *Bruce and Young's theory of face recognition, including case studies and explanations of prosopagnosia*

The specification requirements are clear: a knowledge and understanding of Bruce and Young's theory is required. You need to be able to both describe and evaluate it. You should also have a working knowledge of case studies and explanations of the visual agnosia, prosopagnosia.

Bruce and Young's theory of face recognition

Face recognition is the process by which human faces are interpreted and understood. It is believed humans have an innate attraction to faces, incurring a survival value as it helps create attachments and allows recognition of people, important for social interactions.

Bruce and Young's is a stage theory, with face recognition involving two different mechanisms.

Familiar faces: structural encoding, followed by face recognition nodes, person identity nodes and name generation.

Unfamiliar faces: structural encoding followed by expression analysis, facial speech analysis and directed visual processing.

For a face to become familiar, it has to be seen several times so that a firm representation is stored. Therefore the structural encoding, based on a pictorial code, improves.

Face recognition is seen as a **holistic** process, where facial features, involving eight independent sub-processes working together, are processed collectively (see

Table 9). Different processing modules are used to process different types of information, for instance facial expression.

Table 9 Sub-components of face recognition

Type of component	Description of component
Structural encoding	Creation of descriptions and representations of faces
Expression analysis	Analysis of facial characteristics to infer emotional state
Facial speech analysis	Analysis of facial movements to comprehend speech
Directed visual processing	Selective processing of specific facial data
Facial recognition nodes	Stored structural descriptions of familiar faces
Person identity nodes	Stored information about familiar people
Name generation	Separate store for names
Cognitive storage	Extra information that aids the recognition process

The theory believes two types of information are held on people:

Visually derived semantic code: details related to physical aspects, e.g. gender, race.

Identity-specific semantic code: biographical details not related to physical aspects, e.g. hobbies, achievements.

Retrieval of information from the identity-specific semantic code permits recognition of faces.

The theory proposes two types of node:
- **Face recognition node** (FRN) containing structural information on faces.
- **Person identity node** (PIN) containing identity specific information.

The theory attempts to explain how facial information is analysed. The recognition of familiar faces is seen to involve matching results of structural encoding and stored structural codes that describe familiar faces, located in the FRNs. Then identity-specific semantic codes are obtained from the PINs so that name codes can be retrieved. Both facial features and the configuration of those features are used to recognise faces as being familiar.

Research
- Ellis et al. (1979) found that external facial features, e.g. hairstyle are used more to recognise unknown faces, while internal features, e.g. nose are used more with familiar faces. However, as only static pictures of faces were used the results may not reflect how face recognition occurs in real life situations.
- Bruce and Valentine (1988) found that expressive movements, such as smiling and nodding, seemed to convey little variant information to aid identification, suggesting that invariant information is used more to perform face recognition.
- Sergent (1984) presented two identikit faces that either differed on one or two facial features, such as shape of eyes or chin. Deciding if the faces were different

occurred faster when they varied on two features, implying that facial features are processed collectively (configural processing) rather than independently.

- Diamond and Carey (1986) found that expert dog breeders were not good at identifying individual members of a familiar breed if the image of the dog was upside down. This indicates that face recognition requires sensitivity to the overall configuration of a face, rather than just sensitivity to the configuration of facial features. However, Shepherd et al. (1981) found evidence that individual facial features are used in face recognition. When describing faces, participants outlined individual features rather than the overall shape, seeming to contradict the findings of the previous study, but participants were asked to merely describe rather than identify faces and description may be easier and different than face recognition.
- Malone et al. (1982) reported on two case studies. The first involved a man who was able to recognise familiar faces but could not match up photos of unknown faces. The second study involved a man who could not recognise known faces but could match up photos of unknown people. The results suggest damage to different brain areas, suggesting that familiar and unfamiliar faces are processed differently, supporting the prediction of Bruce and Young's model.
- Young et al. (1985) investigated the theory's prediction that as FRNs and PINs are separate types of store, then if just a FRN was activated, the person should seem familiar, but we would not be able to provide any information about them. Participants kept a diary of problems in recognising faces and the results showed clear support for the prediction, supporting the theory.

Evaluation

- The theory has led to predictions being made, which research has generally found to be true, thus supporting the theory.
- The theory is backed up by case studies of visual agnosias (see case studies of prosopagnosia for details) that face recognition consists of independent sub-components.
- The theory's central idea that face recognition is a holistic process and consists of a series of independent stages is generally accepted, lending support to the theory.
- The theory's belief that familiar and unfamiliar faces are processed differently is backed up by research evidence, again supplying support for the theory.
- The theory states that the processing of facial information should occur in a sequential fashion and again this is supported by evidence, backing up the theory.
- The theory has led to the development of practical applications; for instance the introduction of computer security systems that use face recognition software.
- The theory is not without criticism. It is not adequately able to explain how unfamiliar face recognition occurs or how familiarity is achieved, therefore weakening support for the theory.
- Many parts of the theory are well explained and have empirical support. But it is not clear exactly how some of the sub-components work in helping to determine face recognition, for example cognitive storage.

- One aspect that is not yet fully understood is the relationship between face recognition and object recognition, although case studies of visual agnosia have shed light on this area.
- Although there is a wealth of research evidence to back up the theory, there is some contradictory evidence too. The theory predicts that names can only be gained from relevant autobiographical information stored in the PINs. However, De Haan et al. (1991) detailed a case study of a patient for whom this was not true, weakening support for the theory.

Case studies of prosopagnosia

Sufferers of visual agnosias, of which prosopagnosia is a type, do not have damage to their visual systems, but cannot use or make sense of certain visual information. Visual agnosias often result from stroke damage to the posterior occipital and/or the temporal lobes of the brain. Sufferers can usually describe objects or faces in terms of their features and colours etc. but cannot name them even if they are familiar.

Originally it was believed that the perception of objects and faces involved processing by the same neural mechanisms. However, case studies of prosopagnosia have generally indicated that there might be a specific processor for faces.

Prosopagnosia is associated specifically with damage to the fusiform gyrus area of the brain. Sufferers can generally recognise objects, but not faces. The fact that there are different types and levels of prosopagnosia indicates that each stage of face recognition can be affected, which gives strength to Bruce and Young's notion that face recognition consists of a sequence of stages. Currently there is no long-term effective treatment for the condition, but hopefully a fuller understanding of the disorder may lead to one in time.

Dailey and Cottrell (1999) have provided an explanation of how a separate face processing mechanism could arise. This is based on the idea of the visual system developing a processing sub-system useful for the recognition of faces, occurring as a natural response to a child's developmental environment, for example a child's need to identify faces from an early age.

Research

- Bodamer (1947) coined the phrase prosopagnosia when reporting on three case studies, one of a man with a bullet wound to the head who could not recognise familiar people or his own image in a mirror. He could however recognise people using other senses such as smell.
- Brunsdon et al. (2006) reported on a boy, AL, who could not recognise familiar or unfamiliar faces, suggesting that his damage was at the level of structural encoding right at the beginning of the face recognition process. This can therefore be used in conjunction with other evidence to suggest that face recognition is composed of sequential stages.
- Kurucz et al. (1979) reported on examples of prosopagnosics who could name familiar faces, but were unable to identify their facial expression. Bruyer et al. (1983) had a patient with the opposite symptoms, namely being able to

understand their facial expressions, but was not able to name them. This suggests, in line with Bruce and Young's theory, that facial expression analysis and name generation are separate components of face recognition.

- Campbell et al. (1986) found a prosopagnosic who could not name familiar faces, nor identify their facial expression, but who was able to perform speech analysis. This provides evidence that facial speech analysis, again in line with the theory, is a separate component of face recognition.
- Lucchelli and De Renzi (1992) reported on a case study where a patient could not name familiar faces, but could give accurate and detailed semantic information about them. This indicates support for the existence of PINs being an independent sub-component of face recognition as predicted by Bruce and Young. As the patient had no problems naming objects or geographical positions, this indicates that face recognition involves a separate processing system from other objects.
- Bredart and Schweich (1995) reported on a prosopagnosic who knew if someone was familiar or not but could not name them or relate any biographical information about them. His long-term memory and ability to recognise and name other objects was fine. He had no damage to his structural encoding as he could recognise if faces were faces and knew if a picture of a face was complete or not. His ability to name facial expressions was also unimpaired. In terms of Bruce and Young's theory he could be seen as having damage that incurred no problems in the early stages of face recognition processing, but had damage that affected later stages, namely accessing PINs from FRNs and with gaining name codes from PINs. This does support the notion that face recognition processing occurs in separate stages.
- Kanwisher et al. (1997) have found neurological evidence to support the idea that face recognition involves a separate processing mechanism. Results from fMRI scans were collected to compare brain activity on presentation of images of faces, scrambled faces, hands and houses. The fusiform gyrus was found to be more active in face recognition than in object recognition, implying that this brain area may be associated specifically with face recognition processing.
- Bauer (1984) found a patient whose galvanic skin response went up when looking at a familiar face and the correct name was read out, suggesting that although face recognition may not appear present at a conscious level, unconsciously it is.

Evaluation

- The fact that evidence shows that generally prosopagnosia affects face recognition in different ways seems to suggest that face recognition does occur as a holistic process of sequential, independent sub-components.
- Prosopagnosia has provided a wealth of research evidence with which to evaluate the worth of Bruce and Young's face recognition theory. However, this evidence comes from case studies, detailed studies of one person. Therefore there is a concern as to how representative these cases are of the general population, especially as they involve cases of people with abnormal brain conditions.

- Evidence from case studies has not always proven straightforward, with examples of contradictory evidence, especially concerning whether face recognition involves a separate processing mechanism.
- Humphreys and Riddoch (1987) have cast doubt on the idea of object and face recognition being processed separately by different mechanisms. They suggest that face recognition may simply be a more complex form of object recognition. If so then slight damage to a general-purpose recognition system would affect object recognition less than face recognition. Backing up this claim is the fact that prosopagnosics do tend to have slight damage to their object recognition ability and severe damage to their face recognition ability. Evidence from case studies has not always proven straightforward, with examples of contradictory evidence, especially concerning whether face recognition involves a separate processing mechanism.
- Gauthier et al. (2000) also cast doubt on the idea of separate processing mechanisms. Faces may just be complex objects that take more skill to recognise. This is backed up by the fact that the fusiform gyrus is activated not only during face recognition, but in object discrimination too. Therefore the fusiform gyrus cannot be specifically involved in face recognition. It was also found that some prosopagnosics have general problems with complex object recognition including faces, suggesting that a specific face processing mechanism might not exist.
- Face recognition involves the cognitive approach, a strength of this is that it is a scientific approach that lends itself to making testable predictions, as occurred with Bruce and Young's theory. However, a weakness is the abstract nature of the approach, as with the sub-components of Bruce and Young's theory, of which there is no proof that they exist in any objective, physical sense.

Gender

Psychological explanations of gender development

Specification content

- *Cognitive developmental theory, including Kohlberg and gender schema theory*
- *Explanations for psychological androgyny and gender dysphoria including relevant research*

As the specification names Kohlberg's cognitive developmental theory there is an explicit requirement to have sufficient knowledge of the theory so that it could be both described and evaluated. A similar requirement is necessary for gender schema theory. Examination questions could focus on either of these two theories or ask you to compare them.

The second requirement of the specification is that you can provide explanations of psychological androgyny and gender dysphoria along with relevant research evidence about them. Again both descriptive and/or evaluative elements may be specified in examination questions.

Cognitive developmental theory

There is a focus on how children's thinking develops, with their thinking being described in qualitatively different stages. Gender identity is seen as the result of a child's active structuring of its own experiences and not as a passive outcome of social learning. Cognitive developmental theory therefore sees thinking and understanding as the basis behind gender identity and gender role behaviour. Kohlberg sees a child as developing an understanding of gender in three distinct stages, with gender role behaviour only being apparent after an understanding has been reached that gender is fixed and constant.

Gender schema theory shares the same cognitive view of gender understanding as Kohlberg but suggests that a child has schemas for gender at an earlier stage.

An important difference between the two theories is that schema theory believes a child only needs gender identity to develop gender consistent behaviours, while Kohlberg sees the acquisition of gender constancy as necessary first.

Kohlberg's (1966) theory of gender constancy

Kohlberg's theory was influenced by earlier theories of cognitive development that saw children progressing through stages of understanding. Gender concepts are seen as occurring through environmental interactions, but these are restricted by cognitive capabilities at a given time. Kohlberg proposed three stages in which a child attains increasingly more sophisticated gender concepts, with a new stage only appearing after thinking has matured to a certain point (see Table 10). Consequently children understand gender differently at different ages, with gender concepts developing as the child actively structures their social experiences. It is not therefore a passive social learning process occurring through observation and imitation.

It is only after **gender consistency** is reached (at about 7 years) that a child can start to develop gender concepts that suit their own gender.

Table 10 Kohlberg's stages of gender development

Approximate ages	Stage	Description
2–3 years	Gender identity	Knowing who is a boy and a girl, including one's self
4–5 years	Gender stability	Knowing that gender is fixed and that boys become men and girls become women
5–7 years	Gender consistency	Knowing that gender is constant regardless of changes, e.g. haircuts, clothes etc.

Research

- Rabban (1950) found, by asking questions about gender, that a child's thinking changes as they age. By 3 years of age most children demonstrated gender identity but did not have an understanding of what they would grow into: a man or a woman. However, by 5 years of age 97% were demonstrating gender stability, backing up the stages of Kohlberg's theory.
- Thompson (1975) found that by 2 years of age a child given pictures of boys and girls could select same sex ones. This demonstrates that the children could self-label and identify the gender of others. By 3 years of age 90% showed gender identity, compared to only 76% of 2 year olds, showing the developmental nature of the concept.
- Slaby and Frey (1975) divided 2–5-year-old children into low and high gender constancy groups. Two films, one of a woman and one of a man performing gender stereotypical activities, were shown side-by-side. High gender constancy children watched the same sex model more. This shows that children of this stage watch their own gender in order to acquire information about gender appropriate behaviour, backing up Kohlberg's notion that gender development is an active process.
- Frey and Ruble (1992) informed children that certain toys were either 'boy' toys or 'girl' toys. Boys who had achieved gender constancy chose 'boy' toys even when they were uninteresting. Girls of the same stage exhibited similar tendencies, but to a lesser degree.

Evaluation

- Kohlberg's theory combines social learning and biological developmental factors to explain how gender development occurs.
- Kohlberg may have underestimated the age at which gender cognition occurs. Bem (1981) believes a child has an awareness of gender and gender specific behaviours from around the age of 2 years, due to the development of gender schemas.
- A child will generally demonstrate gender appropriate behaviours and reward gender appropriate behaviours in peers before they have reached gender constancy, casting some doubt onto Kohlberg's idea of universal stages of development.
- The theory tends to concentrate on cognitive factors and therefore may be overlooking important cultural and social influences, such as parents and friends.

Gender schema theory: Martin and Halverson (1981), Bem (1981)

This is an alternative theory to Kohlberg, but still a cognitive one. Children are seen as developing gender concepts by cognitively processing information from their social interactions. This leads to the construction of **gender schemas**, an organised grouping of related concepts. So once a child has a basic gender identity, it starts to accumulate knowledge about the sexes and organises this into its gender schema, which in turn influences behaviour. **In-group schemas** are formed concerning attitudes and expectations about your own gender, as well as **out-group schemas** about the other gender. This leads to favouring your own gender by spending more time with same-sex peers and actively ignoring anything to do with the other gender.

Toys, games and even objects become categorised as 'for boys' or 'for girls'. The result of this schema formation is the participation of a child in same-sex activities and the beginnings of gender consistent behaviour, with gender stereotypes being reinforced due to only being exposed to same-sex concepts through your social interactions. Therefore the theory predicts that in addition to the development of gender understanding there will be an increase in sex-specific behaviour.

Research

- Martin and Little (1990) found that pre-school children tended to have developed strong gender stereotypes about what was appropriate for boys and girls, before they had developed much understanding about gender, supporting the idea of the formation of gender schemas.
- Masters et al. (1979) found that children aged between 4 and 5 years of age selected toys by their gender label (boy toy/girl toy), rather than by which gender was seen playing with the toy, again indicating the formation of gender schemas.
- Campbell (2000) tested infants aged between 3 and 18 months and found that even the youngest ones had a preference for watching same-sex babies. By 9 months of age boys showed an increasing tendency to pay attention to 'boy toys'. This shows that children from an early age pay more attention to their same-sex group, supporting the idea of gender schemas forming at an early stage of development. This trend is more noticeable in boys.
- Poulin-Dubois et al. (2002) asked 2–3-year-old children to choose a doll to carry out stereotypical male or female jobs. Girls of 2 years of age tended to select the gender appropriate doll, suggesting a schema for gender appropriate tasks. By the age of 2½ years boys were also demonstrating the behaviour, showing that young children are learning from models on the basis of their own sex.
- Martin and Halverson (1983) asked children to recall pictures of people and found that children under the age of 6 years recalled more gender consistent ones, e.g. a male footballer, than gender non-consistent ones, e.g. a male nurse. This is in line with gender schema theory predictions.
- Aubry et al. (1999) performed a longitudinal study into preferences for gender related articles. It was found that once a belief had taken hold that an item was for the opposite sex a reduced preference for that item developed, implying that gender schemas do affect behaviour. The benefit of longitudinal studies is they show trends.

Evaluation

- Gender schema theory offers a plausible compromise between social learning and cognitive developmental theories.
- The theory can explain why children's attitudes and behaviour concerning gender are so rigid and lasting. They focus on anything that confirms and strengthens their schemas and ignore behavioural examples that contradict them.
- The theory neglects the influence of biological factors, as it assumes all gender orientated behaviour is created through cognitive means.

- The theory predicts that as a gender schema develops a child should exhibit behaviour consistent with its perception of its own gender. Some research does show this, but there is contradictory evidence too. Campbell et al. (2002) found that 2-year-old boys and girls who possessed high levels of gender knowledge did not display a preference to play with gender specific toys.
- When a child performs an activity not normally stereotypical of their gender, for example a boy cooking, they adjust their thinking so that the activity becomes acceptable. This implies that thinking can be affected by behaviour, while cognitive schema theory predicts the opposite, therefore weakening support for the theory.

Explanations for psychological androgyny

Traditionally individuals are seen as being either masculine or feminine, but the concept of psychological androgyny involves having both male and female characteristics. This can generally be regarded positively, as it allows an individual to choose the most appropriate behaviour. An individual may act masculine in some situations and feminine in others, or may blend together elements of both.

Bem (1975) developed the androgynous hypothesis, which saw androgyny as being a positive and desirable condition.

Olds (1981) believed that androgyny was a developmental stage reached by only some people. Bem (1983) argued that androgynous individuals have a different cognitive style and can adopt behaviours, when necessary, which are independent of gender concepts. Therefore in terms of cognitive schema theory androgynous people are **gender aschematic**, in line with Old's explanation, as an individual can only become androgynous when they perceive the world without gender stereotypes.

Orlofsky (1977) has a behavioural explanation for androgyny, seeing it as behavioural style learned by reinforcement, allowing individuals to acquire masculine and feminine qualities applicable to different situations. Therefore androgyny is seen more in behavioural than cognitive terms.

Research
- Bem (1974) devised the Bem Sex Role Inventory (BSRI) to measure androgyny. It consists of masculine, feminine and neutral items that have to be rated by an individual, their score being used to determine their gender personality. 34% of males and 27% of females were found to be androgynous.
- Flaherty and Dusek (1980) found that androgynous individuals have higher degrees of self-esteem, a better sense of emotional well-being and have more adaptable behaviour, backing up the idea of psychological androgyny being positive and desirable.
- Peters and Cantrell (1993) found that androgynous females had the best quality of relationships, supporting the idea of androgyny being a positive condition.
- Kurdek and Siesky (1980) found that androgynous characteristics were seen positively in the workplace, again suggesting that it is a positive condition.

- Burchardt and Serbin (1982) have found that being androgynous scores well in mental health terms, with typically lower levels of depression, although masculine personalities scored equally well.

Evaluation

- Androgyny is not always a positive trait; an individual may exhibit negative masculine and/or feminine behaviours in a given situation.
- Androgyny is perceived as being psychologically healthier, but Whitley (1988) found that having a traditional masculine identity led to higher self-esteem than being androgynous. Zeldow et al. (1985) found that both men and women who scored high on masculinity were better adjusted individuals.
- The BEM scale uses items consistently judged as being either masculine or feminine. However, the ratings for these were done by students and may not reflect those of the general population.
- A criticism of the BSRI is that many masculine traits are seen as positive and female ones as negative. The Personal Attributes Questionnaire (PAQ) deals with this by using only positive feminine and masculine traits.
- Old's explanation that androgyny is a higher stage of development fails to explain how or why this occurs in certain individuals.

Gender dysphoria

Gender dysphoria is classed as a psychiatric disorder and occurs where an individual feels uncomfortable with their biological gender to such an extent that they may wish to change it. Prejudice and negative feelings of anxiety and distress can be experienced leading to depression, self-harm and even suicide. It tends to affect males more than females and it is estimated that 1 in 11,000 people have the condition. Indications of the condition may occur fairly early, with children unhappy wearing clothes of their biological gender, or playing gender stereotypical games. Later behaviour may involve assuming the gender role of the desired sex. Masculinising or feminising hormones can be taken to alter physical features, with the ultimate remedy being gender-reassignment surgery.

Research aimed at explaining gender dysphoria have centred on case studies of diagnosed sufferers and longitudinal studies of individuals identified in childhood as being at risk.

Psychological explanations centre on maladaptive learning experiences, maladaptive cognitive processes and psychodynamic fixations occurring in childhood development. However, biological explanations have become increasingly favoured and centre on the idea of an individual's genetic sex not matching their gender. This is seen as occurring during pregnancy, through additional hormones present in the mother, or by insensitivity to the mother's hormones (androgen insensitivity syndrome) leading to the development of female genitals, but with male genes.

Research

- Wallien and Cohen-Kettenis (2008) performed a longitudinal study that studied a group of gender dysphoric children. At around 19 years of age about 40% of those followed up were still gender dysphoric and these were the individuals who exhibited more extreme symptoms. These individuals also tended to have a homosexual or bisexual orientation, indicating that the majority of children exhibiting gender dysphoria only do so in the short term and that there is an association between being homosexual/bisexual and having childhood gender dysphoria.
- Zucker et al. (2008) performed a longitudinal study on gender dysphoric females referred to a clinic between 2 and 3 years of age. Only 12% were still gender dysphoric at age 18. A study on equivalent males found 20% still had the condition as adults, again suggesting that the majority of people exhibiting gender dysphoria do so only in the short term.
- Rekers (1995) reported that of 70 gender dysphoric boys none had evidence of biological causes but there was a common factor of a lack of stereotypical male role models, suggesting a psychological cause to the disorder, however the majority of evidence does indicate biological causes.
- Kula and Slowikowska-Hilczer (2000) performed a meta-analysis of studies and found that animal studies indicated sex hormones present during pregnancy influence sexual behaviour in adulthood, suggesting that hormones affect masculinisation and feminisation of a child's brain in the womb. This was backed up by another finding, that in individuals with abnormal genitals caused by hormone imbalances, their biological sex and gender identity did not match, again suggesting that hormones may be playing a key role in the development of the condition.
- Hare et al. (2009) examined gene samples from male gender dysphorics and non-dysphorics. A significant correlation was found between gender dysphoria and variants of the androgen receptor gene, implying that the gene may be involved in a failure to masculinise the brain during development in the womb, again giving support for a biological explanation.

Evaluation

- Research in this area is often dependent on case studies, but such a method is often affected by memory bias and selective recall.
- Individuals with the condition often do not perceive it as a disorder, but believe that gender characteristics are a social construction with no relation to biological sex.
- When researching on individuals who are classified as having a mental disorder care must be taken not to cause psychological distress to people who may, by the nature of their condition, be already distressed and vulnerable.
- Although gender confusion in childhood can indicate gender dysphoria, only a minority will exhibit the condition into adulthood.
- Increasingly evidence is suggesting that the influence of hormones and genetics may be responsible for gender dysphoria. However, this is a somewhat simplistic view and

because research studies have not shown distinct result patterns, it is probable that many other interacting factors may contribute to the condition.
- Identification of genes possibly associated with the condition, have caused concerns about foetal gene screening, with a view to aborting 'at-risk' pregnancies.

Biological influences on gender

Specification content

- *Role of hormones and genes in gender development*
- *Evolutionary explanations of gender roles*
- *Biosocial approach to gender development*

The specification outlines the requirement to study three biological areas relating to gender roles and gender development. Each of these is a separate sub-topic in itself and so an examination question could centre on just one specific area, although parted questions could require focus on more than one area.

The biosocial approach and evolutionary explanations are specifically named and so must be studied, as there might be an explicit requirement to address them in examination questions. Similarly there is a particular reference to the role of genes and hormones and they too could form the specific requirement of a question.

Role of hormones and genes in gender development

Many of the physical and behavioural differences between males and females are biological ones. Biological sex is determined by the sex chromosomes X and Y, with an XX combination for a female and an XY combination for a male. Sex chromosomes contain genetic material that control development as a male or female. During this process sex hormones are produced that direct the majority of sexual development. The SRY gene on the Y chromosome controls whether gonads become ovaries or testes, only if the gene is present will testes appear. Testes produce hormones called androgens that prevent development into a female form.

One important androgen is testosterone, which when released causes the development of male sex organs and acts upon the hypothalamus, without this the brain would develop as a female type. Testosterone has been associated with masculinisation of the brain, such as development of brain areas linked to spatial skills. Similarly the female hormone oestrogen plays a role in feminising the brain.

There are differences in the hypothalamus of males and females, with the **sexual diomorphic nucleus** considerably bigger in males and it is believed that these differences may occur through the action of sex hormones, although this is not a universal view.

During puberty testes and ovaries play an important part in determining secondary sexual characteristics that distinguish men from women.

Research

- Money and Ehrhardt (1972) found that a sample of girls whose mothers had taken drugs containing androgen during pregnancy exhibited male type behaviours, such as playing energetic sports and an absence of female type behaviours, such as playing with dolls. This suggests that male hormones can have a strong influence on gender behaviour.
- Koopman et al. (1991) found that mice that were genetically female, but lacked the SRY gene, developed into male mice if the gene was implanted into them, demonstrating the important role the SRY gene plays in determining gender
- Young (1966) gave male hormones to female mice and female hormones to male mice. The effect was a reversal of usual gender related behaviours, suggesting that hormones have a key role in determining gender behaviour. However, there is the problem of generalising to humans from animal studies.
- Berenbaum and Hines (1992) conducted a study on girls suffering from congenital adrenal hyperplasia, a condition where high levels of male hormones cause the development of large female genitalia. The participants were much more interested in male activities than sisters who did not have the condition, implying that male hormones have a masculinising effect on the brain during pregnancy.
- Hines (1994) found that girls with congenital adrenal hyperplasia, although seeming to prefer playing with boys, did not show significant differences in the amount of rough and tumble play from girls without the condition. This contradicts the findings of Berenbaum and Hines.
- Deady et al. (2006) conducted research on women who were not mothers. It was discovered that there was a significant correlation between high testosterone levels in saliva and a low desire to have a family, suggesting that a female's maternal drive may be linked to hormone levels.

Evaluation

- Research evidence consistently shows that biological factors are important in gender development, although the influence of social factors needs to be considered too.
- Research has tended to indicate associations between hormones and gender related behaviour. However, this does not show causality and other factors may be involved. Davies and Wilkinson (2006) have found evidence that genes may also be involved in producing the masculinisation and feminisation of the brain.
- If biological factors were responsible for sex differences, then it would be expected that these would be apparent from an early age. However, there is little evidence of early behavioural differences between males and females. Therefore differences that appear later may be explicable to some extent by social factors.
- Ethical concerns must be considered when performing research on people with abnormal conditions, such as congenital adrenal hyperplasia. Such participants are especially vulnerable to distress and psychological harm. A cost-benefit analysis may help to decide if such research would be beneficial.

Evolutionary explanations of gender roles

Most human evolution is thought to have occurred in the EEA due to selective pressures and the behaviour that is exhibited now is actually a product of that time.

Males and females are believed to have evolved different gender role behaviours due to different adaptive pressures.

Mating strategies: males produce millions of sperm and can theoretically fertilise lots of females, incurring little cost to themselves. However, they cannot be certain of paternity. Females have far fewer opportunities to become pregnant and incur high costs when they are. However they can be certain of maternity. Therefore adaptive pressures have led to gender behaviour differences, with men seeking to impregnate as many fertile women as possible and women seeking genetically fit males who will invest in them and their offspring. Physical aggressiveness is seen between competing males, which is possibly why males have evolved to be bigger and stronger and females also compete to be seen as more attractive.

Pair bonding: evolutionary theory explains the existence of monogamous pair bonding as occurring due to its advantages for both sexes. Females get protection and resources for themselves and their children, while males can ensure sexual fidelity and a good degree of paternal certainty.

Adaptive advantage of sex roles: the development of sex roles in humans brought with it an adaptive advantage. Men hunted and women, with child caring duties, farmed and prepared food. This led to the creation of bigger social groups and an ability to avoid starvation. Neanderthals became extinct, possibly because they did not have such gender roles.

Gender roles: differences in behaviour between the sexes may be due to evolution. Women are restrained by child caring duties and men possess greater physical strength. Therefore women can only conduct behaviours that are consistent with nurturing children and men can conduct behaviours that require mobility and power.

Interpersonal sex roles: females are more nurturing and this has an evolutionary advantage in threatening situations, where a female's responsibilities would lie in caring for the children. For males, as the hunters, the better response is one of flight or fight.

Research
- Wood and Eagly (2002) conducted a cross-cultural study comparing gender behaviours in different societies. Characteristic of non-industrial societies was men hunting and killing animals. Men manufactured tools while women looked after children, collected and cooked food, suggesting that gender behaviours have their origins in evolution.
- Zeller (1987) found that although some activities were perceived as being exclusively male or female, there were many other activities that were seen as

being applicable to either sex, such as milking, manufacturing and harvesting food. This weakens the evolutionary explanation.

- Tamres et al. (2002) found that in times of threat and stress, women tend to seek the company of others much more so than men, supporting the idea that interpersonal sex roles have been naturally selected by evolution.
- Buss (1989) conducted a survey that gathered information about mate preferences from 37 cultural groups. Females tended to seek males with resources and ambition, while males sought physical attractiveness much more than females and desired younger partners, supporting the idea that mating strategies have evolved differently between the sexes due to different environmental demands. The idea that men would place more importance on chastity was only supported to a small extent, casting doubt on the explanation.
- Holloway et al. (2002) investigated the idea of males being larger in order to compete for females (and impress choosy females). It was found that human males tend to be 1.1 times bigger than females, but in chimpanzees, where pressures for male competition are more intense, males tend to be 1.3 times bigger, strongly supporting the idea of gender size differences being due to evolutionary pressures.

Evaluation

- The evolutionary approach is criticised by some as being deterministic in seeing gender differences as biologically inevitable.
- Evolutionary theory provides a plausible explanation for the physical differences that exist between males and females and also why men tend to be more promiscuous and women more choosy in their sexual behaviour.
- One problem with cross-cultural studies, often used to judge predictions based on evolutionary theory, is that samples are different, which can cast doubts on the validity of the results
- Even if gender roles have evolved, it does not necessarily mean that they have positive outcomes. For example men can be negatively affected by feelings of jealousy and rejection.
- Although, as predicted by evolutionary theory, many traditional male activities require strength, so do some typically female activities, such as carrying water and food. However, evolution may have shaped women to perform activities that could be carried out in conjunction with child rearing.

Biosocial approach to gender development

Biosocial theory sees gender as being determined by both biological and social factors working in conjunction with each other to produce masculine and feminine behaviours and identities. Therefore gender cannot be explained by biology alone, for instance psychological androgyny and gender dysphoria indicate that biological sex does not necessarily reflect gender.

Biosocial theory believes it is the perceptions of biological sex that lead to gender identity and gender role behaviour. A newborn baby is labelled as male or female and this labelling has consequences for how the child will be perceived and treated, with boys and girls being treated differently, for example how they are handled. So gender can be seen as being socially constructed and therefore differing across cultures and over time.

While biological explanations see gender behaviours as being exclusively due to biology and therefore fixed and constant, the biosocial model sees them as being much less rigid. This means that it should be possible for a person to change and develop in ways that are not confined by traditional views of male and female behaviour and identity.

Research

- Money (1975) reported on one of a pair of identical twins who had gender re-assignment surgery to turn him into a girl because of accidental, irreparable damage to his penis. The boy was given female hormones and raised as a girl. It was reported that at 9 years of age she had a female gender identity, although some male behaviour was seen too, suggesting that gender identity can be achieved through social means and that rather than being biologically determined, we are 'gender neutral' at birth. However, ultimately, when told of her life history she reported never having been happy as a female and opted for re-assignment surgery to become male once again, suggesting that for individuals with a clear biological sex, gender identity is biologically determined.
- Bradley et al. (1998) reported on a similar case of a biological male that, after accidental damage to his penis, had re-assignment surgery and was raised as a female. This individual had exhibited some male behaviours as a child, but preferred female company and as an adult, felt female and was happy that way. This particular case study does suggest that biological sex does not determine gender identity.
- Smith and Lloyd (1978) dressed babies in non-specific gender clothes and then either labelled them with a boy or a girl's name. It was found that people would play with them in different ways according to their gender label, with 'boys' treated in a much more physical manner. This is in line with biosocial theory, which explains that the gender label would direct how the child would be perceived and treated.
- Wetherell and Edley (1999) offer support for the biosocial view that gender behaviour is flexible. They found several different styles of adult masculinity being exhibited by men, such as unconventional, sporty and 'new man', indicating that gender role is not fixed exclusively by biology.

Evaluation

- Studies of individuals being given re-assignment surgery and raised as the opposite gender to their biological sex have produced contradictory results and have been prone on occasion to researcher bias. For instance Reiner and Gearhart (2003) reported on 16 biological males born without a penis, given re-assignment surgery and raised as females. All exhibited male tendencies and 10 decided to become male again by 16 years of age. Money (1991) however, reported on 250 cases of people being happy with gender re-assignment. Clear conclusions therefore have not been possible.

- Early gender related behaviours appear to be more biologically directed, Kujawski and Bower (1993) found that 1-year-olds prefer to watch same gender children, suggesting that initially innate factors dominate.
- The fact that the model sees gender behaviour as not solely innate and fixed, means that it should be possible for an individual to develop their gender identity into new and positive ways.
- Ideas about gender seem to differ cross-culturally and this suggests that gender roles and behaviours are a social construction.
- The biosocial model is an example of how psychological approaches can work in unison and should therefore not be seen as single, exclusive explanations of human behaviour.

Social contexts of gender role

Specification content

- *Social influences on gender role, for example the influence of media, parents, peers and schools*
- *Cross-cultural studies of gender role*

The specification focuses upon social influences, but those named are only done so as examples and so they would not be specifically required in an examination question, therefore it would be perfectly acceptable to use any other relevant social influences. There is a wealth of research evidence to utilise both for descriptive and evaluative purposes.

There is an explicit requirement to have a working knowledge of cross-cultural studies of gender, but as no specific studies are named any relevant ones could be used as source material to answer an examination question.

Social influences on gender role

Parents

Parents have an important role to play in reinforcing children's gender behaviour due to their expectations of what is and is not appropriate. Therefore when a son or daughter demonstrates what is perceived as gender appropriate behaviour, it will be reinforced by rewards of praise and attention. Parents can act as gender role models too, demonstrating gender appropriate behaviours for their children to observe and imitate. Children may also, by a gradual process of immersion, be taking on their parents' own gender schemas.

Research

- Lytton and Romney (1991) found that parents reinforced with praise and attention stereotypical gender behaviours in both boys and girls, for example the activities they participated in, suggesting that social environmental factors do play a part in determining gender behaviour. However, children were also raised quite similarly in many ways, suggesting that reinforcement alone cannot account for the development of gender behaviours.
- Eccles et al. (1990) reported that children were encouraged to play with gender stereotypical toys by their parents, supporting the idea that parents reinforce gender roles.
- Fagot and Leinbach (1995) compared children raised in 'traditional' families where dad went to work and mum cared for the children, with ' alternative' families, where mum and dad shared the child caring. At 4-years-old the children were given gender labelling tasks as a means of testing their gender schemas. The 'traditional' family children displayed more gender role stereotyping and used gender labels earlier, suggesting that parents do act as gender role models for their children.
- Tennebaum et al. (2002) conducted a meta-analysis that examined the degree of relationship between parents' gender schemas and their children. A significant positive correlation was found, which suggests that parents may influence gender development by means other than reinforcements and acting as role models.

Peers

Peers have a strong social influence by acting as role models, with children more likely to imitate same sex models. Peers also help to reinforce gender stereotypes, for example by praising gender appropriate clothes and ridiculing non-appropriate ones.

Research

- Archer and Lloyd (1982) reported that 3-year-old children who played the opposite sex's games were ridiculed by their peers and ostracised, supporting the idea that peers police gender roles.
- Lamb and Roopnarine (1979) found evidence of peers rewarding sex appropriate play in pre-school children and ridiculing sex inappropriate play, demonstrating the strong influence peers have in reinforcing gender behaviour.

Schools

Schools can exert social influences in several ways. First teachers may moderate parent and peer influences by reinforcing less gender stereotypical attitudes and behaviour, but they may also enforce gender stereotypes, for example through separate dress codes for boys and girls. Teaching materials can also exert an influence. Primary school teachers tend to be female and this may explain why boys do comparatively worse as they perceive learning to be for girls.

In secondary education there is a tendency for men and women teachers to teach gender stereotypical subjects, for instance men teaching maths and pupils regard subjects as either being 'girl subjects' or 'boy subjects'. Again these influences are reinforced and policed by parents, peers and teachers.

Research

- Renzetti and Curran (1992) reported that teachers gave reinforcement in the form of praise to boys for instances of 'cleverness', while girls received praise for 'neatness', supporting the view that teachers enforce gender stereotypes.
- Colley (1994) found that in secondary schools, pupils had a tendency to view individual subjects as either masculine or feminine, demonstrating that social influences on attitudes and beliefs about gender are apparent in schools.

Media

The media is seen as being a strong social influence on gender behaviour by portraying gender stereotyping and reinforcing gender appropriate behaviours and attitudes. This may occur through social learning theory, where children observe and imitate stereotypical gender models on television and in books, or by cultivation, where the more television is watched, the more the child's perception of the world comes to resemble what they see on television.

Research

- Williams (1986) found that children who view a lot of television, where the content tends to be gender stereotypical, have much more traditional beliefs about gender roles, suggesting that the children are acquiring gender beliefs through observation and imitation.
- Peirce (1993) conducted a content analysis of teenage girl's magazines. Girls tended to be portrayed as weak and reliant on others, with a focus on being in a relationship rather than having independent aspirations, demonstrating the influence of the media in establishing gender attitudes and behaviours.
- Leaper et al. (2006) found that animated cartoons showed males and females in gender stereotypical ways. Males were more aggressive and females more fearful, showing that there are a wide range of media influences affecting gender development.

Evaluation

- Children tend not to imitate behaviour they see being rewarded that does not 'fit' their gender. For example a boy will not imitate a girl's behaviour they see being reinforced. Instead they only imitate behaviours fitting their gender stereotypes, implying that cognitive and social factors are involved.
- Social learning theory, by the use of observation and imitation of role models, cannot explain the acquisition of gender behaviours alone as patterns of reinforcement are not uniform. However, it does have some part to play.
- Studies that have looked at the influence of the media in determining gender roles can only establish associations, but not causality as other factors may be involved. For instance a child may choose programmes that suit its gender beliefs.
- Peers may have a stronger role in reinforcing gender roles than parents, because peers police gender behaviours, for instance, by ostracising those who indulge in non-stereotypical behaviour.

content guidance

- Parents seem to have more influence over children's gender concepts and behaviour when they are young, but peers become more important as gender role models in later childhood.
- The fact that children respond in a selective manner to reinforcement suggests that cognitive factors may be important in influencing gender behaviour. Fagot (1995) found that teachers try to reinforce female behaviours in boys and girls but that only girls learn them.
- If social learning can lead to children developing traditional views on gender roles and behaviour, then it should be able to deconstruct them. Johnston and Ettema (1982) showed 12-year-olds episodes of a television programme designed to counter gender stereotypes and indeed both boys and girls exhibited reduced stereotyping.
- Williams (1985) reported on a town that had previously not had television. After 2 years it was noticeable that children's attitudes to gender roles became much more stereotypical, demonstrating the power of the media as a social force in establishing gender attitudes.
- A lot of research into the development of gender involves children under 16 years of age. This presents problems in gaining informed consent, which must be gained from parents or guardians and not just teachers.
- Media influences on gender development may have been exaggerated, because a lot of gender development occurs before 4 years of age when media influences are not great. In later years media influences probably reinforce existing gender beliefs rather than create them.

Cross-cultural studies of gender role

The thinking behind cross-cultural studies is that if similarities were found in gender roles across cultures, this would suggest that they are biological in nature, while if differences were found then it would suggest that they were socially constructed.

Research

- Mead (1935) conducted research into gender differences between various tribes in Papua New Guinea. In one tribe, the Arapesh, both males and females exhibited gentle, caring personas. In another, the Tchambuli, the men exhibited what would be regarded in Western culture as female behaviours, while women exhibited traditional male behaviours. In a third tribe, the Mundugumor, both exhibited aggressive personalities. This seems to indicate that gender roles are socially constructed rather than being biological in nature. There is the possibility of researcher bias in interpreting the behaviours exhibited and Mead did subsequently change her views, believing instead that gender behaviours can be biological in nature.
- Whiting and Edwards (1988) researched into various cultures' gender attitudes and behaviours and found that it was fairly universal for girls to be encouraged into domestic and child caring roles, while boys were assigned tasks involving responsibility, for instance looking after animals. This suggests it is the activities they are given to do that are responsible for the differences in gender roles.

- Williams and Best (1990) looked at attitudes to gender roles in different cultures. It was found that there was universal agreement across cultures about which characteristics were masculine and which feminine, with men being perceived as dominant and independent and women as caring and sociable. The researchers also found that children from these cultures exhibited the same attitudes. The implication is that attitudes to gender roles are universal and therefore biological in nature.
- Barry et al. (1957) performed research across many non-Westernised cultures, looking at which qualities were deemed important for males and females. Nurturing was seen as a dominantly feminine characteristic, while self-reliance was seen in the same way for males. These findings reflect those from Western cultures and therefore suggest a biological basis to gender roles.

Evaluation

- Globalisation may be contributing to the lessening of cultural differences and there has been a reduction in the differences between masculine and feminine gender roles, implying that social influences are stronger than biological ones.
- A methodological problem with cross-cultural studies is that it is difficult to obtain identical samples and there can be problems with researchers being biased in terms of their own cultural viewpoints.
- The findings from cross-cultural studies can be related to the nature–nurture debate. If gender roles, behaviours and attitudes are found to be universal, then this suggests that they are innate and due to nature, while if cultural differences are found, then this is more indicative of nurture influences.
- Collectivist cultures seem to hold much clearer views about which gender roles are male and female than individualistic cultures.

Questions
&
Answers

This section contains mark band descriptors and sample questions in the style of Unit 3. Each question is accompanied by guidance explaining the question's requirements, followed by a sample answer and examiner's comments and marks, detailing the strengths and weaknesses of each answer and explaining how the marks were awarded. Examiner's comments are preceded by the icon ℮.

Theories of intelligence

Outline and evaluate psychometric theories of intelligence. (25 marks)

AO1 credit is gained from outlining relevant theories and to meet the demands of the question at least two theories must be provided. Remember that if more than two were provided, less detail is required. Only 9 marks are available for the outline, so the majority of time and effort should be spent evaluating the theories. This could be achieved by building an effective commentary upon the amount of research support that the theories have and considering any practical applications that have arisen. Using theories other than psychometric ones would only be a creditworthy strategy if they were to be used as a comparison.

■ ■ ■

Candidate's answer

Spearman used factor analysis to find the two basics parts to intelligence. One was general intelligence, called 'g'. This is involved in all mental tasks and everybody has it, but in different amounts. This is the type of intelligence that IQ tests measure. The second type was specific intelligence, called 's'. This type concerns specific skills that only certain people have. Spearman thought that 'g' was more important because it showed the differences between people. He also thought 'g' was innate and fixed at birth. There has been some suggestion that 'g' may actually be related to how efficient a person's nervous system is.

Spearman's theory was important, because it provided the impetus for intelligence testing by IQ tests. It also focused interest onto studying intelligence and factor analysis became an established research method in psychology, such as in the study of personality. Johnson and Bouchard (2005) using factor analysis claimed to have discovered a single, higher order factor of intelligence and this seems to indicate that general intelligence does exist. However, Kitcher (1985) disagrees and thinks there is no single measure of intelligence that we can all be compared on and that therefore general intelligence does not exist. Spearman's theory was never popular and was replaced by more multi-factor theories such as Guildford's.

Guildford was working to find a selection method for pilots. He rejected the idea of there being a general intelligence factor and thought there were 120 separate mental abilities. He arrived at this figure by using factor analysis to conclude that there were five types of operation, four types of content and six types of product. You multiply these together to get 120 abilities. He then set out to try and create tests that would measure each ability.

Many of the scores individuals achieved on Guildford's tests were similar, suggesting that they may actually be measuring the same thing and that therefore there are not 120 separate abilities. His theory has proven practical applications in education, for instance the Structure of Intellect (SOI) teaching programme. This identifies a student's weaknesses and strengths and allows for a personal learning strategy to be constructed. It has wide ranging applications, being used with those who have learning difficulties, as well as gifted students. Bradfield and Slocumb (1997) provided support by finding that SOI created better critical thinkers. Although intended as a theory of intelligence, Guildford's theory has shown itself to have practical applications in other areas, such as personnel selection, career counselling and employment training programs.

One big problem with psychometric theories is that their use of factor analysis, if truly objective, should produce an agreed number of basic factors. However, the fact that it produces figures as wide ranging as Spearman's two factors and Guilford's 120, seems to indicate it is not as scientific and accurate as it claims. One possible explanation for this is the different types of participants that were used in research. Spearman used schoolchildren who, by their very nature, have wide differences in levels of intelligence. Guildford used college students who tend to have intelligence levels that are closer together. This sampling difference in their methodology may have led to them finding different numbers of basic factors.

A major issue with psychometric theories concerns the nature–nurture debate, as the theories tend to assume that intelligence is innate in origin, unaffected by environmental factors and thus remains constant, making it measurable. People are then tested and selection for things such as jobs and schooling are justified on the results of these tests. But, there is a lack of convincing evidence that intelligence is actually innate, which casts doubts on these applications.

This is an excellent answer. It is relevant, informative and accurate. It is well constructed, with the majority of time and effort being dedicated to constructing evaluative material. Remember that is where the majority of the marks are available.

Two valid psychometric theories are offered and the candidate uses the strategy of first outlining a theory, then evaluating it before moving on to do the same with the second theory. Both outlines are in the top band of marks, showing a good range of relevant material, with the knowledge used being both accurate and detailed, with a good deal of depth and clarity. Guildford's notion of operations, contents and product is presented in a list-like fashion and could perhaps have been better described.

The evaluation also achieves the top band. Relevant research evidence is provided and there is substantial evidence of coherent elaboration, with the points made being built up into an effective commentary throughout. The candidate provides analysis and evaluation specific to the two theories used and then moves on towards the end to provide more general evaluation of psychometric theories in general, even utilising the useful practice of comparing the theories with each other. Material concerning the nature–nurture debate and its relevance to psychometric theories is clearly documented, satisfying the need to include such material in order to gain access to the higher bands of marks.

(AO1 = 8/9) + (AO2 = 15/16) = 23/24 marks

Animal learning and intelligence

Discuss the evidence for intelligence in non-human animals. (25 marks)

AO1 credit could be gained by detailing explanations of animal intelligence, such as the research evidence concerning social learning, self-recognition and Machiavellian intelligence. Again as the majority of marks (16) are available for AO2/AO3 material then most effort should be spent on evaluating evidence. This could be achieved by considering the extent to which research does or does not support the idea of intelligence in non-human animals. Constructing a commentary based upon the difficulties in actually determining intelligence in animals could also prove effective, such as the difficulties in assessing whether behaviour is due to learning or to an animal's biology. It should be remembered that, as in all Unit 3 questions, there is a need to include material on issues/debates/approaches, for example the ethical considerations when conducting research with animals.

■ ■ ■

Candidate's answer

Intelligence in animals concerns their abilities to learn and process information. Research has looked at three areas: social learning, self-recognition and Machiavellian intelligence.

Social learning concerns what animals learn through their interactions with each other and several types have been identified. First, imitation where behaviour is observed and then copied, second, stimulus enhancement where attention is directed onto a part of the environment to help it learn how to find the solution to a problem, third, emulation where an animal learns to reproduce the consequences of modelled behaviour. These first three types of social learning are passive, or accidental, because the animal being copied does not deliberately set out to teach the behaviour. There is a fourth type, tutoring, which is an active type as the model deliberately sets out to teach.

Whiten found that chimpanzees living in different colonies imitated ways of eating ants that were specific to their colony. Nagell found that a type of monkey learned to clean potatoes before eating them, because they had their attention focused onto the dirty potato and seawater to wash it with. This is an example of stimulus enhancement. Tomasello found some monkeys who watched another monkey using a rake to get food. They used a rake too, but with their own particular method. This is an example of emulation. Rendell and Whitehead reported on killer whales who act as tutors by delaying the killing of seals so that their children could practice hunting skills.

question

Mirror tests have been done to see if animals can recognise themselves by touching a dot painted on their face when they were unconscious. Gallup found that primates can do this and other researchers have found lots of animals and birds that can too.

Machiavellian intelligence occurs when animals deceive and manipulate others. Nishida showed that alpha males share food with non-rivals so that they will help out with power struggles.

A lot of this research is done with wild animals and for such research to be ethical the researchers must not lower the animals' fitness in any way. They would lower their fitness if they restricted their access to food or mating opportunities or harmed them in any way to get their results. There is another potential methodological problem when researching on animals and that is interpreting their behaviour. Researchers might be guilty of researcher bias and unconsciously interpret their data in a way that lends support to their hypotheses. For example if a researcher believes that animals can be tutors, then she might mistakenly interpret their behaviour in that way.

With social learning there are not very many examples known of tutoring, so it has not really been proved that it exists. With self-recognition the mirror test might not really be a good way to test if animals actually do have the ability, because not all animals use sight a lot, for instance dogs use smell more. Dogs cannot self-recognise with the mirror test, but they can recognise their own scent. Examples of Machiavellian intelligence may not be all they seem too, because they might actually be examples of responses conditioned through reinforcement that have happened in the past.

This is a good answer. The content of this answer is accurate, relevant to the question and presents a good amount of detail. There is evidence of breadth too, as the candidate provides material on several forms of social learning as well as self-recognition and Machiavellian intelligence. Indeed the descriptive part of this answer is excellent, with a thorough knowledge and understanding of the topic area clearly displayed. Relevant research examples are given for most areas covered and no marks are lost for not presenting the dates of the research, indeed it is worth remembering that with positive marking credit can never be lost, but only gained.

However, the failing of this essay is that too much time and effort is spent compiling the descriptive part of the answer. Only 9 marks are available for this, while 16 are on offer for the evaluation.

There is some evaluation and it is all creditworthy, but what there is, tends to be fairly basic, with little evidence of elaboration. It would have been a good idea and easy to achieve, if this candidate, when describing research studies, had gone on to make some related evaluative points, for instance by using key AO2 statements such as 'this suggests that...' or 'this is supported by...'

There is some material concerning issues, namely the difficulties and concerns when researching with wild animals and this is of better quality, if a little long-winded at times.

Another good way to gain AO2/AO3 credit would have been to create an effective commentary on the ability of bird species to self-recognise, for example Prior's work with European Magpies and evaluate what this tells us about intelligence in such animals.

(AO1 = 9/9) + (AO2 = 8/16) = 17/25 marks

Evolution of intelligence

(a) Outline cultural influences on intelligence test performance. (5 marks)

(b) Outline and evaluate evolutionary factors in the development of human intelligence. (20 marks)

Part (a) of this question requires purely AO1 description. Including an evaluation of material on cultural influences on intelligence test performance would gain no credit and take away from valuable examination time better spent elsewhere. As only 5 marks are available, be careful not to offer too much material, as it would not earn any extra credit.

Part (b) requires both description and evaluation of evolutionary factors, but there are only 4 marks available for a brief outline, so be sure to concentrate most efforts on the evaluation. This could be achieved by assessing the extent to which research supports the idea that intellectual capacities have evolved and by considering the strengths and limitations of such evidence, for example the difficulties involved in assessing hypotheses based on evolution.

■ ■ ■

Candidate's answer

(a) One cultural influence is that of cultural bias in IQ testing. IQ tests have generally been designed by and standardised upon people from a white culture. This means that they contain questions based upon white culture and so quite clearly people of other cultures are often at a disadvantage. Another cultural influence is that of poverty. People from non-mainstream cultures tend to live in poorer environments and this negatively affects performance on IQ tests. Brooks-Gunn (1996) found that over half the difference in IQ performance between white and black children was due to poverty. People from minority cultures often lack motivation and stimulation to learn material tested by IQ tests, again disadvantaging them.

(b) There are several factors that have been associated with the development of intelligence. Ecological demands, where humans have to be able to hunt, find food and use tools to survive and thrive. Social complexity is where humans living in groups need intelligence to deal with the conflicts of group living and increased brain size due to a need for manual dexterity and increased ability to process information.

Research has generally supported the idea that intelligence has evolved. Boesche (1992) tested out the idea that a need to use tools and cognitive skills in order to find embedded (hidden) food caused intelligence to evolve. It was found that chimpanzees used tools to open nuts in a manner remarkably similar to archaeological evidence from early human nomads of East Africa. The nomads lived in a harsh environment, developing elaborate tool use to find embedded foods in order to survive. The fact that chimpanzees had developed the ability is strong evidence that intelligence has evolved, though there is a problem in interpreting the meaning of animal behaviour.

Not all evidence is so supporting though. Dunbar (1992) investigating the idea that fruit eaters would need to have evolved high intelligence to find occasional fruits, found no meaningful relationship between the amount of fruit in an animal's diet and the size of its cortex, which does not support the hypothesis. However, an animal might only need small amounts of fruit to obtain vital minerals and vitamins, so Dunbar's conclusion may be wrong. Fruit-eaters tend to have larger brains than leaf-eaters. Leaves are more abundant, but less nutritious, suggesting that the ecological demands of foraging led to increased intelligence. However, the hypothesis does not explain why fruit eaters would need such a diet. Did they need energy from fruit to fuel their larger brains, or did the brain need to grow to develop the cognitive abilities to locate fruit?

One of the problematic issues with evolutionary theory is the difficulty in assessing hypotheses based on the approach. Evolutionary theory has also been criticised for being reductionist, reducing behaviour down to just one factor, that of adaptiveness.

Holekamp and Engh performed research supporting the idea that the demand of social living brings a need for a larger cortex and advanced abilities in social cognition. They found that as the complexity of social living increased so did the brain size of carnivores and that hyenas, which live in large, complex groups, had an advanced cognitive ability to recognise dominance relationships between other group members.

This is an excellent answer. Part (a) of this question is answered well. The candidate does not fall into the trap of providing evaluation, which would gain no credit. Instead cultural influences that relate to intelligence test performance are accurately and concisely outlined and the candidate has been careful not to produce too much material, which would have gained no extra credit.

In part (b) there is a need to keep the outline brief as only 4 marks are on offer and the need to outline evolutionary factors associated with intelligence has clearly been met. However, the answer is a little 'list like' and perhaps a bit more detail would have been advisable.

Sensibly the majority of the answer is concentrated on the evaluation and an effective commentary is built up around the central idea of foraging hypotheses, especially how they relate to frugivores. Pertinent points concerning the evolutionary approach itself are made and a concise, but informative evaluation of Holekamp and Engh's important research is detailed. One point worth noting is that in the outline relevant reference to increased brain size was made, but no evaluation of this area is made. However, there is no requirement to do so and the candidate has concentrated on providing

question

appropriate evaluative points in other areas. In examinations, with constraints of time, it is often not possible to cover all areas that we would ideally like to.

A last consideration is the lack of material concerning methodological evaluation of studies used to consider evolutionary factors in the development of human intelligence and this has reduced the overall mark.

(AO1 = 5/5 + 3/4) + (AO2/AO3 = 13/16) = 21/25 marks

Eating behaviour

(a) Outline factors influencing attitudes to food and eating behaviour. (9 marks)

(b) Evaluate explanations for the success and failure of dieting. (16 marks)

The descriptive and evaluative parts of this question are nicely divided into two clear parts. However, remember that they concern two different areas of eating behaviour. Therefore, part (a) should only contain an outline consisting of brief details relating to factors that have an influence over attitudes to food and eating behaviour, such as mood, health concerns and cultural factors, while part (b) should purely be an evaluation of explanations concerning the success and failure of dieting, with consequently no description of the explanations required. To achieve this, focus could be upon determining whether research findings support explanations, what the strengths and limitations of these findings are and a consideration of assessing what constitutes success and failure in dieting.

■ ■ ■

Candidate's answer

(a) Food is vital and there are several things that influence our attitudes and what we eat. Mood is important, as the emotional state we are in has been found to influence eating behaviour. A researcher gave grapes and popcorn to participants who had to watch either a sad film or a comedy. Those watching the sad film chose popcorn, presumably to try and make themselves happy, while those watching the comedy chose grapes, presumably to prolong their contented mood. Another researcher discovered that people who went on food binges had increased negative moods, suggesting a practical application in that junk comfort foods need information stickers to warn depressed people about the dangers of binge eating.

Culture also plays a part. Different cultural eating practices are transmitted to group members and culture can either have a direct or an indirect influence. Some researchers found that cultural groups, who believe eating well is important, eat healthy food.

Health concerns also affect attitudes and eating behaviour. A researcher got participants to put factors taken into account when choosing food into rank order. The sensory qualities of food, such as its taste and appearance was ranked above health concerns, seeming to indicate that eating healthily is not the most important factor in determining eating behaviour

(b) Dieting involves deciding to cut intake of food and most people have been on a diet. They do not tend to work though, because weight lost is soon put back on. A successful diet is one where at least 10% of body weight is lost and kept off for at least one year, but only 20% of dieters achieve this target.

There are several explanations for dieting success and failure. Motivation plays a part, either by reinforcement, like money, for losing weight, or by using social support to help a dieter achieve their target. Researchers found that offering money for weight loss did not work, as participants did not lose a lot of weight or keep it off, suggesting that financial incentives are not a good motivator. Other researchers found that 71% of members of Weight Watchers, a slimming group that encourages the use of social support to lose weight, kept off a weight loss of at least 5% of body weight, suggesting that social support works as a motivator to successfully lose weight.

It has been found that behaviours common to losing weight involve a low-fat diet, monitoring food and weight and doing more exercise.

Diets usually fail because they are impossible to stick to. Motivation declines because of the stress of feeling hungry all the time and people lose their focus and abandon their diet. Researchers found that people who cannot concentrate well tend to lose their focus on what they're trying to achieve and the methods they're supposed to be sticking to and therefore their diet fails. This suggests that cognitive factors have a role to play in whether diets are successful or not. Explanations of success and failure in dieting should perhaps be considered collectively rather than individually.

This is a moderate answer. Three relevant factors are outlined in part (a) and these are generally accurate and reasonably detailed with a good range of material being used. There is a coherence and structure to the answer too. However, two points stand out. First, the candidate has, on two occasions provided an evaluation that this question does not call for. Suggesting a practical application to research into mood and eating behaviour incurs no credit, nor does evaluating the relative importance of health concerns. Time would have been better spent on outlining more descriptive material. Second, the outline at times requires more detail if access to a higher band of marks is to occur. For instance it is not really clear what is meant by culture having a direct or indirect influence.

The content of part (b) does concern explanations of success and failure. However, the majority of time the candidate merely describes reasons for failure and success, but does little in the way of evaluating them. The answer also starts off with a general outline of what dieting actually is, an approach that does not attract credit. What is required is an evaluation of the value of the various explanations and this is achieved occasionally, for example using evidence to show that cognitive factors may have a role to play and that providing social support is a successful form of motivation. The only other creditworthy comment occurs at the end, concerning the possible need to consider explanations collectively, although this point is not well made.

To gain more marks the candidate could have used more research evidence in an evaluative fashion, either by suggesting what an analysis of the evidence tells us, or by commenting on methodological or even ethical concerns. Material on possible practical applications could have been presented and an effective commentary could have been constructed around factors such as individual differences. There is a need to include material on issues/debates/approaches if the mark earned is to be above the basic mark band descriptor.

(AO1 = 5/9) + (AO2 = 6/16) = 11/25 marks

Biological explanations of eating behaviour

Outline and evaluate evolutionary explanations of food preference.   (25 marks)

Like all examination questions this one is taken directly from the specification but care must be taken to shape the selected material to the specific demands of the question, rather than just describing and evaluating evolutionary theory.

Therefore, an outline is required that focuses upon describing how food preferences, such as those for sweet tastes, may have arisen due to evolutionary adaptations occurring as a response to environmental demands. The more important evaluative part of the answer could be centred on the extent to which research supports or goes against this idea, although it might also be a useful strategy to include commentary based upon the difficulties of conducting research that effectively assesses the value of evolutionary theory. Inclusion of material on issues/debates/approaches could be orientated around the reductionist and/or deterministic nature of evolutionary theory.

■ ■ ■

Candidate's answer

Evolutionary theory explains that food preferences evolved due to environmental demands through natural selection and therefore bestow an adaptive advantage. The evolution of human food preferences occurred in the EEA, reflecting our need for energy, to avoid toxins and to store excess calories as fat for times of scarcity.

Sweet tastes indicate high-energy and non-poisonous content and were naturally selected to become a preference. Steiner (1979) looked at neonates' food choices and facial expressions, concluding they innately prefer sweet tastes, though the results may be prone to researcher bias and Beauchamp (1982) found that this preference becomes modified by experience fairly quickly, showing the importance of both nature and nurture in determining preferences. Many animals prefer sweet tastes, supporting the idea of an evolutionary preference. However, the explorer Stefansson (1960) found that Copper Eskimos, who lived exclusively on meat and roots, were repulsed by their first taste of sugar, indicating it's not a universal preference.

De Araujo et al. (2008) used genetically modified mice that could not taste sweetness and found they preferred sugar solutions rather than non-calorific sweeteners, implying that we have a preference for calories rather than sweetness.

The fact that people exhibit different levels of the preference may be due to genetic reasons. Zhao et al. (2008) believes variations in sweetness preference are due to the variability of genes in individuals, suggesting the variability is not due to cultural factors.

Bitter tastes indicate toxins and have evolved to be avoided. Mennella (2008) found children have a greater sensitivity to bitterness than adults, indicating that the preference is innate with environmental factors moderating it over time. The findings are supported by the fact that children generally avoid bitter tasting vegetables and refuse bitter medicines. A practical application of this research would be to make such medicines sweeter tasting.

Simmen and Hladik (1998) found humans have many receptors for bitter tastes, but only a few for sweet tastes. This seems to suggest that it is more important to avoid toxins than to ingest calories. You can always find another meal, but you cannot recover from death.

The ability to detect bitterness may be declining in humans. Go et al. (2005) found more pseudogenes in humans than other primates, seeming to indicate that the preference is modified by environmental changes, suggesting that evolution is an ongoing process and relevant to modern life.

Humans also have an evolved preference for salt, which is essential for survival. Dudley et al. (2008) reported that ants in areas with low salt levels prefer salty solutions to sweet ones, compared to ants in salt-rich environments, suggesting the preference has evolved and is linked to adaptive fitness. Beauchamp (1983) found that people with sodium deficiencies have an innate desire to eat more salt, find it tastier and can tolerate it at high concentrations, suggesting that there is an evolutionary controlled mechanism maintaining sodium levels through salt ingestion.

Zinner (2002) found that 23% of neonates exhibit a preference for salt and had higher blood pressure than average and at least one grandparent with hypertension, a condition linked to high salt intake. This indicates there may be a genetic basis to salt preference that explains individual differences in its prevalence.

🖉 This is an excellent answer. It is a high-quality, concisely written, relevant, informative essay with elements of both breadth and depth. Research evidence is used in both descriptive and evaluative fashion and there is substantive evidence of understanding and organisational structure. The answer is well focused with coherent elaboration, points being built up to form an effective commentary. There is some reference to issues/debates/approaches, for example the nature–nurture debate and to methodological considerations, for example the risk of researcher bias. However, these areas would benefit from some enhancement.

(AO1 = 9/9) + (AO2 = 13/16) = 22/25 marks

Eating disorders

Discuss two biological explanations for one eating disorder. (25 marks)

Neural and evolutionary explanations are the two biological explanations named on the specification and would therefore form the basis of most candidates' answers, although any other relevant biological explanations would be perfectly acceptable. Description of two biological explanations would form the AO1 content of the answer, with care being taken to not include psychological explanations, as these would not be creditworthy. The two biological explanations offered could be evaluated individually in terms of how much support they have from research studies and whether they can be used to form effective treatments, or biological explanations collectively could be assessed with psychological explanations possibly being introduced as comparison.

The explanations used both in terms of descriptive and evaluative content would have to be centred on just one type of eating disorder, as the question specifically demands this. Using two or more eating disorders would result in only the best one being credited.

■ ■ ■

Candidate's answer

Obesity is an increasingly prevalent eating disorder and attempts have been made to explain it by reference to biology.

One such explanation is neural factors. The hypothalamus is a part of the mid brain associated with the control of hunger and appetite. The ventromedial hypothalamus (VMH) has been identified as the satiety centre and the lateral hypothalamus (LH) as the hunger centre. Two theories have been put forward: dual control theory and set-point theory. There is evidence to support both theories, but set-point theory is more favoured. Evidence from post-mortems on obese people shows damage to the VMH, suggesting that neural factors cause obesity. However, such post-mortems are rare and hard to generalise from and most obese people probably do not have a damaged VMH.

What is likely, as Friedman (2005) reports, is that two neurons called POMC and NPY regulate appetite and thus body weight. The hormone leptin also has a role, but leptin injections do not really work, so maybe it is not that important. Genetics may also play a part.

Another biological explanation comes from evolution. Most evolution took place during the EEA when often food would be scarce. Therefore we evolved to like fatty foods, because they contain lots of energy and extra was stored as fat for lean times. We now live in a world where there is always high calorific food and because of evolution we eat as much as possible, laying down a lot of fat. Maybe this explains obesity. Maybe also we put on weight when we eat foods that we did not used to eat, as our body does not know how to handle them. Bray states that lots of American drinks are sweetened with corn syrup, which was not part of our evolutionary past and the increase in its use has matched the increase in obesity, suggesting that corn syrup production does not stimulate leptin, which normally dampens down our eating and thus we get fat. This was supported by DiMeglio and Mates (2000), finding that participants put on more weight when given calories in liquid form than solid form, suggesting that we have not been shaped by evolution to cope with liquid calories.

Evolution gives us a believable explanation for obesity, because it explains that we are not designed to cope with the modern world of ever-available food and put on the excess as fat. Some however, accuse the approach as being determinist, because it only sees a role for biology, but actually it does acknowledge that environment plays a part.

A problem with the biological approach is that it often researches on animals and the results might not be generalisable to humans. They also tend to be laboratory based and thus artificial.

✍ This is a reasonable answer. Some parts are relevant but there is irrelevant material too, such as that concerning dual control and set-point theory, which would attract no credit. At times material is not explained fully enough to convey knowledge and understanding, for instance it is not explained what the role of leptin is, or what role genetics play. There are some parts however where research is used coherently to form part of a reasonably effective commentary, for example the material on the role of liquid calories in developing obesity. There is also a reasonable presentation of evaluative material on the evolutionary approach. Overall the answer is generally focused, with reasonable detail at times, but little in the way of elaboration.

(AO1 = 5/9) + (AO2 = 9/16) = 14/25 marks

Theories of perceptual organisation

Describe and evaluate Gibson's bottom-up (direct) theory of perception. (25 marks)

Gibson's theory is specifically named on the specification and so you are required to have studied it. Nine AO1 marks are available for an account of the theory and a careful consideration of whether research studies support this view of perceptual organisation could form an effective method of assessment. Gregory's theory could be used as a means of evaluative comparison (but would not earn any AO1 descriptive credit) and the influential nature of Gibson's theory could be stressed along with the theory's strengths, limitations and practical applications. The inclusion of material on the nature–nurture debate could also be incorporated to help gain access to the higher bands of marks.

■ ■ ■

Candidate's answer

Gibson worked for the US air force and his interest in perception came from training pilots. He thought that in the vast, ever changing barrage of sensory information received by the body's sensors, which he called the optic array, there was sufficient information to allow direct perception without any need for processing at a higher level. Therefore perception occurs in a 'bottom-up' fashion, building perception from the sensory data itself. Gibson thought that perception therefore was innate and had been shaped by evolution as it has an adaptive survival value.

One reason sensory information is so rich is because we move around in our environment and features of the environment are in motion too, giving a dynamic source of information to perceive from. Certain features of the optic array are seen as being constant. These are called invariants and permit direct perception.

One type of invariant feature is optic flow patterns. These are unambiguous sources of information, such as height and distance. Optic flow patterns contain the depth cue motion parallax, where as we move about in our environment, more distant objects appear to move more slowly than nearer ones.

Another invariant feature is texture gradients. These are surface patterns that contain sensory information about depth and shape and so forth. Motion parallax is present again as movements occur, as is the depth cue of linear perspective, where parallel lines appear to converge as they get further away, like train tracks for instance.

A third type of invariant feature is horizon ratios, which concerns the position of an object in relation to the horizon. For example objects of varying size at the same distance from an observer will appear to have different horizon ratios.

The final type of invariant feature is affordances and this is where meaning is attached to sensory information. Affordances are the action possibilities of an object: what you can do with it. For instance a toothbrush 'affords' cleaning your teeth.

Support for the theory came from Bardy who found that participants walking on a treadmill that had a screen, onto which optic flow patterns were transmitted, kept their balance by using motion parallax to perform balancing movements. They were able to do this by using invariant information in the optic flow patterns, indicating that direct perception from optic flow patterns is possible as predicted by Gibson's theory.

Further support came from Frichtel, who showed a film of a car driving through scenery and 4-month-old children were able to use texture gradient to perceive, suggesting that perception is innate, supporting the idea that direct perception is possible without learning experiences.

Creem-Regehr also provided support when he restricted participants' viewing conditions and found that they were able to judge distance by using invariant horizon-ratio information. This suggests that, as Gibson states, direct perception is possible from invariant sensory information.

Empirical backing for the concept of affordances came from Warren who gave participants of differing sizes various images of staircases with different heights of steps. Participants were able to 'afford' whether a staircase could be climbed by a person of their size, giving some support to Gibson's theory, although it's hard to believe that we would know what all objects are for without some learning experiences.

Gibson's theory is a good theory, but can only explain perception when viewing conditions are ideal and therefore permit perception directly from the sensory information. When viewing conditions are ambiguous or incomplete, Gregory's theory is better.

This is a good answer. The candidate chooses the strategy of first describing the theory and then evaluating it. This is a decent enough strategy, but has caused the candidate to produce an unbalanced answer, in that there is more descriptive material than evaluative and yet more marks are available for evaluation. Only by practice can you really hope to get this right. The descriptive material is sound and accurate and a good range of material is evident, with a coherent structure. Maybe a more concise writing style would allow for the same quality of descriptive material, but in a shorter amount of time and words. This again is something that can be practised.

The evaluation is centred, quite legitimately, on research studies and these are well used, drawing out the pertinent points to show whether Gibson's theory is supported. Overall the evaluative part of the answer is reasonable, although elaboration is generally at a minimum and reference to issues/debates/approaches are only at the lower end of being reasonably effective. Evidently time constraints have curtailed the time spent on evaluation.

(AO1 = 9/9) + (AO2/AO3 = 9/16) = 18/25 marks

Development of perception

(a) Outline what is meant by the nature–nurture debate in relation to explanations of perceptual development. (5 marks)

(b) Outline and evaluate infant studies of the development of perceptual abilities. (20 marks)

Part (a) of this question requires an outline of the nature–nurture debate. However, this outline must be focused upon explanations of perceptual development (and nothing else) in order to gain credit. Bear in mind that as only 5 marks are available care must be taken not to provide too much material, as such an approach would not earn extra marks.

For part (b) the specification states a specific requirement for infant studies to be covered and therefore you should have a wealth of relevant material to select from to earn the 4 AO1 marks on offer. The majority of the marks (16) are available for the evaluation and so most time and effort should be concentrated here, so it's important not to spend too long merely describing studies. Evaluation could take the form of whether research studies provide support for perceptual abilities being innate or learned, whether the findings of research studies are supported by other studies, methodological considerations of specific studies quoted and of infant studies in particular. A consideration of the ethics involved when researching with infants would be a relevant issue to include.

■ ■ ■

Candidate's answer

(a) The nature–nurture debate is a philosophical argument, centred in this case on whether the ability to perceive is inborn in us or is learned.

As perception is not a single ability, but a set of different skills that go together to create perception, it may well be that some perceptual skills are more innate in nature, while others are more learned. The more complex skills may be more environmentally determined, as they need environmental experiences to be fully developed.

Another feature of the nature–nurture debate relevant here, is that of interactionism, where innate and environmental factors work together to create perceptual abilities. So early perceptual skills necessary for survival are more innate and are developed into more complex skills by learning experiences.

(b) Gibson and Walk became interested in depth perception when they visited the Grand Canyon and then made a model with a piece of non-reflective glass covering an apparent vertical drop. They wanted to see if newborn animals and 6- to 14-month-old babies would cross over the apparent cliff. Young animals would not and neither would 92% of the babies, even when called over by their mothers, which was a bit stressful.

Campos (1970) used the same experimental method as Gibson and Walk, but used 2-month- and 9-month-old babies, measuring their heartbeats. When a 2-month-old baby was taken across the apparent deep side of the model, its heart rate tended to decrease, but when a 9-month-old baby was moved across its heart rate increased.

Sen (2001) tested neonates' ability to perceive depth. The babies had an eye patch over one eye and were presented with a visual illusion of a revolving hooped cylinder, where one end of the illusion appears nearer to the observer. It was found that 7-month-old babies, but not 5- to 6-month-old babies, would reach for the seemingly nearer end of the illusion.

Imura (2008) performed research testing whether neonates had shape constancy. This was achieved by examining their sensitivity to shading and line junctions. Computer generated pictures were presented to children aged between 5 to 8 months. First they were given a pair of picture displays, where one switched between two-dimensional and three-dimensional images and the other one switched between two two-dimensional images. The results were that the older children spent longer looking at the two-dimensional–three-dimensional images, while the younger children did not show any differences in time spent looking.

Bower (1966) examined neonates' ability for size constancy. Children aged between 6 to 8 weeks were used and they were trained to look at a 30-centimetre cube one metre away by being tickled and played with when they looked at it. They were then given several other sized cubes at varying distances:

(1) A 30-centimetre cube at a distance of three metres, producing a smaller retinal image than the original stimulus.

(2) A 90-centimetre cube at a distance of one metre, producing a retinal image three times larger than the original stimulus.

(3) A 90-centimetre cube at a distance of one metre, producing a retinal image the same size as the original stimulus.

How many head turns a baby did to each stimulus was recorded and option (1) had the most with 58 head turns, followed by option (2) with 54 head turns and then option (3) with 22 head turns.

This is a moderate answer. In part (a) the nature–nurture debate is explained and more importantly is explained as it relates to perceptual development, which is what the question requires. The central idea of some perceptual skills being possibly innate and others more learned is explained in terms of the debate, as is the idea of nature–nurture influences working upon each other. The answer is thorough, accurate and coherent and earns the full marks available.

8

question

Unfortunately examiners see far too many answers like this candidate's attempt at part (b). The question required an outline and evaluation of infant studies relating to perceptual development, all the material produced is relevant to the question asked but is purely descriptive in that it merely outlines studies in terms of their aims, procedures and findings. The material produced is accurate and often well detailed and so scores excellently for the AO1 marks available. However, the only evaluative comment in the whole answer is a passing reference to ethical concerns. This is a shame as this candidate obviously knows a lot about the topic and if they could acquire some evaluative skills then their mark would go up dramatically. This could be achieved by using research studies to assess their effectiveness, in terms of the conclusions reached, the methodology used, any practical applications that arise and so forth. For instance the Bower study could have been used to suggest that size constancy is innate and does not require learning experiences. This could then be related to the nature–nurture debate and an effective commentary easily achieved in terms of ethical concerns when testing infants and the methodological problems associated with research in this area.

(AO1 = 5/5 + 4/4) + (AO2/AO3 = 1/16) = 10/25 marks

Face recognition and visual agnosias

'Prosopagnosia is a form of visual agnosia where generally familiar objects can be recognised, but not faces.'

Discuss the extent to which case studies of prosopagnosia support the idea that face recognition occurs through a separate processing system. (25 marks)

The term 'discuss' means there is a requirement to describe and evaluate. The question also specifically states the need to concentrate on studies of prosopagnosia. Therefore description of such studies would be necessary in order to form a relevant outline. Evaluation needs to address the question of whether research findings lend support to face recognition occurring through a separate processing system. A balanced evaluation could easily be created, as there is evidence for and against this idea. The contradictory nature of some of the evidence and the methodological problem of generalising from case studies could also form part of an effective analysis.

■ ■ ■

Candidate's answer

Case studies of prosopagnosia have become of interest to psychologists, because they are an effective means of examining how face recognition occurs in humans.

As prosopagnosia has been associated with damage to a specific brain area, the fusiform gyrus, speculation has grown that face recognition involves a separate processing mechanism from recognition of other objects.

Prosopagnosia generally involves impairments in the ability to recognise familiar faces, while the ability to recognise other objects is unaffected, suggesting the existence of two separate processing mechanisms for faces and objects.

Lucchelli and De Renzi (1992) reported on a case study who could not name familiar faces, both people known personally and famous people. However, the patient's ability to put names to other objects and geographical locations was unimpaired, suggesting that face recognition has its own processing mechanism, as presumably the prosopagnosia caused brain damage to the area associated with processing faces, but not the area processing other objects.

Kanwisher et al. (1997) found neurological evidence supporting the existence of a specific face recognition processor. Measurements were made using fMRI scans of brain activity to present images of whole faces, scrambled faces, houses and hands. Greater activation in the fusiform gyrus brain area was recorded during face recognition than object recognition, suggesting that face recognition has a separate processor. However, Righi and Tarr found evidence that the fusiform gyrus is involved in other than just face recognition.

Gauthier et al. (2000) backed up this criticism, finding that the fusiform gyrus was active when participants were asked to discriminate between types of birds and cars. The researchers believe that faces are complex objects that need more skill and practice to recognise, explaining why there is more activation during face processing. But the fact that there is activation, albeit to a lesser degree during other object recognition goes against the idea of separate processing mechanisms.

Gauthier et al. (1999) presented evidence suggesting that faces are processed under the same mechanisms as other objects. They reported that not all prosopagnosics have specific problems in recognising faces, but have general problems with complex object recognition. However, this only occurs with a minority of cases.

One general problem is the methodology of case studies. Such cases are rare and there is a concern with how representative the results are, especially as they concern people with an abnormal brain condition. Another problem is the unreliable nature of the findings. Case studies have produced conflicting results, making it difficult to ascertain whether separate processing mechanisms exist or not. There are also ethical concerns over using people with brain damage as research material, though a cost-benefit analysis might suggest such research is legitimate as it may lead to the formation of effective treatments to address the condition.

Humphreys and Riddoch (1987) doubt that faces and objects are processed differently. They feel that recognition of faces is a complex form of object recognition. If true then slight damage to a general-purpose recognition system would affect object recognition less than face recognition. Evidence backs this up, as prosopagnosics do generally tend to have severe damage to their face recognition abilities and slight damage to their object recognition capabilities.

However, Dailey and Cottrell (1999) have provided an explanation of how a specific face processing mechanism may have arisen in response to our early developmental environment. Because recognising faces is important from an early age to make attachments, recognise friends and strangers etc. then perhaps our visual system, during development, creates a processing sub-system dedicated to face recognition, suggesting a plausible reason for the existence of a specific processor.

Face recognition involves the cognitive approach and a weakness of this is the abstract character of a lot of the subject matter. A strength however, is its scientific nature and ability to make testable predictions. With face recognition, the prediction of there being a specific processing mechanism is not generally supported.

🗹 This is an excellent answer. The material is relevant, accurate, coherently expressed, detailed and contains elements of both breadth and depth. The reasons why a specific processor may exist are stated and explained and research evidence is used not only in a clear descriptive manner, but as an efficient form of evaluation too. The contradictory nature of the evidence is discussed and criticisms used in such a way as to form an effective commentary. Both ethical and methodological considerations are explored in a pertinent manner and the cognitive approach itself is also drawn into the discussion in an illuminative manner. Finally and possibly most importantly, this candidate has struck a correct balance in determining what proportions of descriptive and evaluative material are required.

(AO1 = 9/9) + (AO2/AO3 = 16/16) = 25/25 marks

Psychological explanations of gender development

Compare Kohlberg's cognitive theory and the gender schema theory explanations of gender development. (25 marks)

Description of Kohlberg's cognitive theory and the gender schema theory would be necessary to earn AO1 credit. Any description of other theories relating to the development of gender would not gain credit.

16 marks are on offer for an evaluation, which, as the question suggests, should be centred on a comparison of the two theories. This could be achieved by assessing the degree of research support and backing there is from other theories and by detailing similarities and differences between the two theories, alongside their strengths and weaknesses. Gender bias could be successfully incorporated as an issue specific to this topic area.

■ ■ ■

Candidate's answer

Kohlberg was influenced by general cognitive development theories that see children's understanding and thinking as progressing through stages. So although ideas about gender are seen as being formed by interactions with the environment, they are restricted at any given time by which stage an individual is in. Kohlberg proposed three stages, each with a more sophisticated understanding of gender concepts, with the next stage not reached until cognitive processes are sufficiently mature.

In the first stage, from about 2 to 3 years, a child develops gender identity and has a knowledge of which individuals are boys and girls, including themselves.

In the second stage, from about 4 to 5 years of age, gender stability is acquired. A child comes to realise that gender is fixed and that boys will grow up to be men and girls to be women. In the third stage, from about 5 to 7 years, gender consistency develops, a child now realising that gender is constant despite any changes in appearance.

Gender schema theory is also a cognitive approach that sees a child acquiring its gender concepts by cognitively processing information gained through social contacts. From this process gender schemas are constructed, which are organised groupings of related concepts. A child therefore gains its gender identity and starts to gather information about the sexes through social interactions, organising these into its gender schema, which in turn directs gender behaviour.

There are in-group schemas about the expected attitudes and behaviours of your own gender and out-group schemas about the opposite gender. Increasingly your own gender is preferred and the opposite gender ignored, with toys and activities being divided up into 'them' and 'us' categories.

The fact that Kohlberg sees children understanding gender differently at different ages, suggests that a child is actively structuring their social experiences and thus it cannot just be a passive social learning process acquired through observation and imitation.

Rabban (1950) gave research support to Kohlberg, finding that children's thinking about gender changes as they grow older. At 3 years children knew their gender identity, but did not know what they would grow into, but by five 97% did. This is in line with Kohlberg's theory. Thompson (1975) supported these findings with similar ones. Two-year-olds knew which pictures were of their gender and the opposite gender, showing they could self-label and label others. By 3 years of age, 90% of children had gender identity compared to only 76% at 2 years of age, showing how children develop their gender understanding with age.

Campbell (2000) found children as young as 3 months had a preference for watching same sex babies and by 9 months boys paid attention mainly to boy toys, supporting the idea of gender schemas forming early on. It would be difficult however to ascertain what a baby so young was looking at or preferred and there is a risk of researcher bias where the researcher unconsciously sees what they want to see.

Overall, gender schema theory, which came later on, is a plausible compromise between gender developmental theory and social learning. However, both theories neglect the influence of biological factors that evidence suggests do have a role to play. Although both theories show the importance of cognitive factors and the cognitive approach in explaining the development of gender roles, they do tend to ignore important social and cultural influences, such as parents and peers.

🖉 This is a good answer. The candidate adopts the sensible strategy of outlining the two theories one after another and although these are generally accurate with a reasonable amount of detail, there is evidence of some repetition and the material would have benefited from being more concise and compact.

The evaluation is achieved by assessing the degree of support each theory has from research evidence and this is done in a reasonable fashion. There is a little evidence of direct comparison of the theories and one way of accessing the higher band of marks would have been to pursue further this type of approach. There is also some evidence of methodological comments and an appraisal of the cognitive approach itself, again this could have been done in a more effective manner. Overall the evaluation is generally well focused and a line of argument is evident, though it is far closer to being basic than effective.

(AO1 = 7/9) + (AO2 = 9/16) = 16/25 marks

Question **11**

Biological influences on gender

(a) Outline the role of genes in gender development. (5 marks)

(b) Outline and evaluate evolutionary explanations of gender roles. (20 marks)

The instruction to 'outline' is an AO1 requirement, so brief details displaying knowledge of the role of genes in gender development would need to be provided to gain credit.

Part (b) also requires a brief outline, this time of how gender roles can be explained in evolutionary terms. Care must be taken to not produce too much descriptive material, as only 4 AO1 marks are available. Therefore most effort and time should be spent producing a relevant evaluation. A good way to achieve this would be to examine the amount of support there is for evolutionary explanations from research studies and to comment on the strengths and weaknesses of such research. Another way of ascertaining whether or not gender roles have been shaped by evolution would be to look at evidence from cross-cultural studies, including details of any methodological problems and inconsistencies in findings as a means of creating an effective commentary.

■ ■ ■

Candidate's answer

(a) Biological sex is determined by genes. Sex chromosomes have genetic material that controls development either as a male or a female. The SRY gene is on the male determining Y chromosome and controls whether a foetus develops its gonads into ovaries or testes. This genetic influence then causes testes to produce hormones called androgens, which stop development into a female. Genes can also occasionally be responsible for abnormal conditions that differ from the norm, for example about 0.2% of men have Klinefelter's syndrome, a genetic condition where their chromosome sequence is XXY rather than the usual XY. They are characterised as being tall, having female-like breasts and being generally infertile.

(b) Differences in human gender roles are explained by evolutionary theory as being due to natural selection, because of their adaptive value. The majority of evolution of gender roles is seen as having occurred during the EEA due to environmental demands of that time. Differences have been documented in mating strategies, pair bonding, gender roles and interpersonal sex roles, all of which are explainable as adaptive responses bestowing evolutionary fitness.

Wood and Eagly (2002) found evidence to support the evolutionary explanation. They found similarities in gender roles in different cultures, for instance men hunting and women cooking, suggesting that gender roles are rooted in evolution. An issue with cross-cultural studies is that samples tend to vary and they can be prey to researcher bias, which may invalidate the results.

Buss (1989) found cross-cultural evidence, supporting the idea that mating strategies have evolved differently to maximise each gender's reproductive fitness. Males seek attractiveness, a sign of fertility, while females seek males with resources, supporting the evolutionary explanation of differences in gender roles. However, the further prediction that males would value chastity more was not proven.

Holloway (2002) found evidence supporting the idea that size differences between males and females result from evolutionary forces. Chimpanzee males are proportionally bigger then human males compared to females of their species. This is in line with evolutionary predictions, as male competition for mates is more intense in chimpanzee circles. Evolutionary theory therefore offers a plausible explanation for why males are bigger: they have to compete with each other for females and choosy females also select this quality as a sign of reproductive fitness, maximising their offspring's chances of survival. However, although many male gender roles do involve the use of their strength, many female activities, such as carrying fuel and food, also require strength, which does not fit easily with the evolutionary explanation. Perhaps evolution has shaped females to be able to perform tasks that can be done in conjunction with child rearing.

Zeller (1987) also found evidence weakening the evolutionary explanation. Although some gender activities were perceived as being exclusively gender orientated, others were performed by both sexes, such as milking and harvesting, not supporting evolutionary predictions.

Evidence supporting evolution comes from Tamres (2002) who found that in response to stress, women seek the company of others more so than men, suggesting that interpersonal sex roles have indeed evolved.

A general criticism of the evolutionary approach is that it's deterministic, seeing gender role differences as being biological and inevitable. Evidence supporting the idea of social and cognitive factors also playing important roles casts doubts on this idea.

This is generally a good answer. The material presented in part (a) is all relevant and fits the question's requirement to only outline the role of genes and not provide any evaluative material. Overall it is reasonably thorough and accurate, but lacks a little in coherence, which reduces the mark slightly.

In part (b) the candidate does not fall into the trap of outlining too much material as there are only 4 marks on offer, instead a general statement outlining the evolutionary explanation of gender roles is given, which is generally accurate and reasonably coherent. The candidate then evaluates the explanation in different ways, by the use of research evidence, ensuring that the material is credited as evaluative by the use of words such as 'suggests' and 'supports'. General evaluative points are made, such as the issue of determinism and the addition of pertinent methodological criticism concerning the use of cross-cultural studies. There is also evidence of an effective commentary being constructed, where the candidate builds upon points with supplementary evaluative points. The major way that this answer could be improved would be to demonstrate more fully at times why certain points were in line (or not) with evolutionary explanations.

(AO1 = 4/5 + 3/4) + (AO2 = 12/16) = 19/25 marks

Social contexts of gender role

Outline and evaluate cross-cultural studies of gender role. (25 marks)

The question is specific in its requirements and answers must be restricted to only providing descriptive details of cross-cultural studies that relate to gender role. There are two main sorts of studies that could be used, those that look for cultural differences and those that look for similarities.

Evaluation of these studies could centre on the degree of support they provide for different theoretical explanations of gender role, for example whether gender role appears to be more biologically or environmentally determined. The inclusion of commentary on the nature–nurture debate would also be relevant to this question. Comparisons of collectivist and individualistic societies in regard to gender role could provide appropriate evaluative material.

■ ■ ■

Candidate's answer

Cross-cultural studies are performed that look for similarities and differences in gender roles. Similarities indicate that roles are innate and biological in nature, while differences support the idea of gender roles being socially constructed. One implication of this is that if gender roles were seen to be biological this would mean that they are fixed, constant and inevitable, while if they proved to be more environmental in origin, this would mean that they could be changed and shaped by learning experiences into gender roles that society perceived as desirable.

A very famous study was that of Mead (1935) who studied three different tribes in the South Pacific. The Arapesh were non-aggressive with both males and females exhibiting traditionally feminine qualities of gentleness and helping with child rearing. The Tchambuli tribe demonstrated opposite gender roles to Western cultures, with the men decorating themselves and flirting, while women made decisions and were more practical. With the third tribe, the Mundugumor, both males and females demonstrated traditional masculine qualities of being aggressive and not very child-centred, suggesting that gender roles are socially constructed and not biologically determined. However, cross-cultural studies are vulnerable to researcher bias. Mead may have been seeing what she unconsciously wanted to see. This criticism is strengthened by the fact that she subsequently (1949) studied cultures in Samoa, changing her views to accepting the existence of cultural similarities. Some have argued that she changed her views due to her marriage to a man with traditional views of gender roles.

It may be the case that due to globalisation pressures cultural differences are lessening, but this may not necessarily indicate biological factors, but instead that similar social influences are shaping gender roles.

Williams and Best (1990) found agreement across cultures as to which traits were masculine or feminine. Men were universally seen as dominant and self-reliant, while women were perceived as caring and group-orientated. This was true also of children in the cultures tested, suggesting that as attitudes are similar, they must be biological in origin. However, Whiting and Edwards (1988) found what was universal was for girls to be encouraged to take on domestic responsibilities, including child-care, while boys were given roles of responsibility in the outdoor environment. So this implies that it is the activities given to males and females that determine gender roles.

The argument about whether gender roles are innate or learned is the central part of the nature–nurture debate and there is evidence to support both views. However, the biosocial theory offers a third possibility that biology and social forces interact together to shape gender roles.

Most studies into gender role have concentrated on Western type cultures with similar influences, which is why comparisons of a wider range of cultures, with differing influences are superior. Barry et al. (1957) carried out a study on 110 non-industrial societies, finding that nurturing was perceived as a dominant feminine quality, while self-reliance was dominantly masculine. These are the same as in Western cultures, implying a biological foundation to gender roles. However, the researchers were from a Western cultural background and may have interpreted the results to suit their own cultural viewpoint.

🖉 This is an excellent answer. It begins with an explanation of the thinking behind cross-cultural studies and an exploration of possible implications of findings. Several relevant studies are outlined in accurate, coherent and detailed fashion with evidence of breadth and depth. Evaluation is well focused with good levels of elaboration and a clear line of argument throughout. Ideas are well structured and expressed clearly, with points being built up in a balanced manner to form an effective commentary. The candidate also makes use of methodological points and the nature–nurture debate in an illuminating fashion, adding further emphasis to the answer.

(AO1 = 9/9) + (AO2/AO3 = 16/16) = 25/25 marks